gestalten

THE ANSWER
to the Ultimate Question of Life, the Universe, and Everything.

When people ask me how many bicycles I have, I have to count them on my fingers. Not because I am so blasé that I forget, but because the number varies depending on the day: my lovely yellow Quintana Roo road bike was stolen in Berlin; my beat-up banger in London disappeared from outside a shop; and I still cannot find the key for my Gazelle in Amsterdam. Newer ones I've added to my collection include a two-gear automatic titanium frame from Velociped, which is too precious to leave out of sight, and a 1970s Fuji Randonneur that I bought from a friend in San Francisco, who made some modifications; it's sporty enough to get around the hills without having to dress up in racing gear.

A lot has changed since the first volume of this series was published. Everywhere, especially in the car-obsessed U. S., bicycles are being recognized for what they always have been: the most efficient way to get around our cities. Covering a distance while getting in some fresh air, exercise, and fun has never been easier. I often beat cars for speed; and battery-support is making moving around town on two wheels even more competitive.

While we still go out for long rides on high-tech road bikes, conquer rough terrain on rugged mountain bikes, and take leisurely vacations with luggage on the back of tourers, the biggest news in bicycles is that, to go from point A to point B, more and more people daily are jumping on the saddle. We're even seeing this shift in places we thought were immune to bicycles, like New York City.

VELO City explores the many changes in the bicycle world, from the practical to the absurd. With so many different kinds of bicycles to choose from nowadays, the optimum number of bicycles to own is still n—1.

Erik Spiekermann
(as of today: 13 bicycles in four cities)

Erik Spiekermann is an art historian, printer, type designer, information architect, author, and cyclist who splits his time between Berlin, London, and San Francisco. Erik founded MetaDesign in 1979, FontShop in 1989, and Edenspiekermann in 2002. He received the Honorary Royal Designer for Industry Britain in 2007 and the TDC Medal & National German Lifetime Achievement Award in 2011. *Hello I am Erik*, a book about his life and work, was published by Gestalten Verlag in 2014. Today, Erik co-runs p98a, an experimental letterpress workshop in Berlin Tiergarten, dedicated to letters, printing, and paper.

COPENHAGENIZE
The bicycle friendly city

obvious choice. Within the metropolitan region, 41% of all trips to work or school are made by bicycle, compared to just 14% by car. From the dense medieval city center to the sprawling suburban industrial parks, residents have come to expect bicycle infrastructure that ensures a safe, easy, and reliable commute. Throughout the citywide network, citizen cyclists enjoy wide cycle tracks on both sides of the streets, synchronized traffic signals, and ample parking.

Copenhagen: A Case Study

Copenhagen made international headlines in 2016 when the number of bikes entering the city outnumbered cars, a clear indication that continuous municipal investment has paid off. Over the past decade, the city has invested $329,140,000 (€268,000,000) in improving bike lanes, facilities, and bicycle bridges. While this may sound like an exorbitant amount, it's less than one of a percent of the budget dedicated to public transportation and private automobiles. In fact, exactly the same price as a single 3 mile (5 km) highway overpass north of the city center, Copenhagen has been able to fund a world class network of bicycle infrastructure for the past 20 years. The economic

Visit the corner of Copenhagen's Dronning Louises Bro and Nørre Søgade, any day, during morning rush hour, and you'll witness a universal sight: a seemingly never-ending stream of sleepy commuters yawning their way to work. Staring off into space, checking their phones, or stealing glances at one another, these everyday commuters are not unlike their counterparts in Paris, Tokyo, or Medellín. The only difference at this particular corner: these residents have all chosen to make their daily trip to work by bicycle, resulting in what might be the most beautiful rush hour in the world.

In the Danish capital, using the bicycle as an everyday mode of transportation has become an

benefits of investing in cycling are not lost on Copenhagen policymakers. A study in collaboration between the municipality and a large engineering firm found that cycling pays off, especially when compared to the private automobile. The study looked at parameters such as vehicle operating costs, time costs, accident costs, pollution and externalities, safety costs, health benefits, discomfort costs, and recreational values. According to the results, for each kilometer driven by car in Copenhagen, society loses $0.93 (€0.76), never to be seen again. Meanwhile for each kilometer

The fact of the matter is that every city on the planet used to be bicycle-friendly.

cycled, society earns $0.22 (€0.18), most of which is enjoyed in reduction in congestion, noise pollution, lifestyle diseases, and vehicle operating costs.

When cycling is approached as an efficient and economically viable mode of transportation, the benefit of investing in its infrastructure is undeniable. It's important to keep in mind, however, that there's nothing particularly Danish about riding a bicycle. The fact of the matter is that every city on the planet used to be bicycle-friendly. From Los Angeles to Berlin, Singapore to Moscow, the bicycle has always been perfectly suited for urban transport. Look

back at vintage photos of streetscapes from the early twentieth century and you'll see city streets populated with horses, trams, early cars, and, of course, bicycles. By that era, the now standardized bicycle (with pneumatic tires, a diamond frame, a chain-driven rear wheel, and identically sized wheels) played an important role in addressing social issues of the time. By design, the bicycle's accessibility opened up new corners of the city for the working class while playing an important symbolic role in women's suffrage movements. Women could now enjoy a sense of

Cities used to be bicycle friendly. Workers on bicycles during the general strike in England, 1926.

mobility previously limited to their male counterparts. The bicycle also opened up new avenues in fashion and politics during the Victorian era. By necessity, women travelling by bike gave up their restrictive and stuffy corsets, petticoats, and skirts for more comfortable bloomers (essentially very baggy pants). Although it didn't happen overnight, this newfound freedom was the beginning of the suffrage movement's rejection of conservative understandings of how and where a woman should be.

"How Many Cars Can We Move Down the Street?"

For thousands of years, our streets were the most democratic spaces in our cities. They were corridors in which raw materials and finished products would travel in and out of our cities. More importantly, they were social and political spaces in which our ancestors played, protested, gossiped, and flirted. This changed in the early and mid-twentieth century, when a concerted effort, backed by the burgeoning automobile industry, was made to redefine our streets. With incredible effectiveness, this effort

redefined city streets through technical solutions coupled with sharp PR campaigns. At the expense of democratic spaces, city streets were handed over to the engineers responsible for modernizing sewer systems and electrical grids. Through the newfound profession of traffic engineering, the issue was approached with a stubborn persistence, implementing a collection of controls and procedures to treat streets as systems to be managed. New laws and social norms emerged, which controlled the behavior of those outside of the car: pedestrians. While laws dictated where and when people could cross the street, good old-fashioned ridicule and name-calling added a sense of shame. Crossing the street in an unsanctioned way in the 1940s, one received the label of a "jaywalker," a colloquial term for a hillbilly or yokel. At the bottom of this twentieth-century effort was one question: how

many cars can we move down the street? As a professional standard, city intersections were now measured by their "level of service," a technical term for how freely cars could pass through. Rather than aim to make streets places where people wanted to be, where parents felt safe letting their children play, and where small businesses could thrive, important decisions were now made based on how well they could serve antisocial interests.

This insatiable appetite for moving as many cars as possible through city streets is a problem that has absorbed traffic engineers for generations. But what have we learned after nearly a century of the practice? The frustrating truth is that, the more roads and highways we build, the more cars appear. This universal phenomenon, known as induced demand, has been observed from Los Angeles to Cairo, as new highways and added lanes intended to relieve traffic congestion seem to fill up within a matter of months.

Intuitive infrastructure keeps things simple. At just a glance, users must be able to easily identify where they belong.

Slow Change

Thankfully, a handful of rational cities are beginning to change the question. Instead of asking how many cars can be moved down the street, these cities come up with a more sensible question: how many people can be moved down the street? By combining a range of transit options, including trams, cars, bicycles, subways, buses, and plain walking, a city street can actually move ten times more people than the conventional traffic model of four car lanes flanked by narrow sidewalks, making the streets not just cleaner and quieter spaces, but incredibly efficient as well.

The bicycle is an important component of any efficient urban street, but to unlock the true potential of the modern and accessible bicycle, streets require proper infrastructure that provides a sense of safety and reliability. With a simple two-and-a-half-meter wide cycle track, more than 5,900 bicycle riders can pass down the street per hour, as demonstrated in some of the great cycling

Newly built bicycle lane in São Paulo, Brazil

cities of the world: Copenhagen, Utrecht, and Amsterdam. Just as with any other legitimate mode of transportation, at the heart of proper bicycle infrastructure are three primary characteristics: intuitiveness, attractiveness, and consistency.

Intuitive infrastructure keeps things simple. At just a glance, users must be able to easily identify where they belong. On a Copenhagen street, you'll instantly know, whether you're traveling by car, bicycle, or foot, exactly where to go. Attractive bicycle infrastructure makes the user feel comfortable and safe. Well-maintained bike lanes wide enough to allow riders to travel at their own pace can also provide a sense of security through physical separation from car traffic. Just as commuters should know exactly what time their train departs each day, residents should be able to rely on consistent bicycle infrastructure. From neighborhood to neighborhood, street to street, residents must be reassured

that they can depend on reliable framework that is maintained year-round. When these conditions are met, cycling becomes an obvious choice for everyday commuters.

While the cities of northern Europe are routinely cited as case studies in bicycle urbanism, examples are springing up around the world. In cities like Buenos Aires, Seville, and Russia's Almetyevsk, where just a decade ago urban cycling would have been a choice reserved for a few hard-core environmentalists and thrill-seekers, the bicycle is now a year-round, everyday mode of transportation, accommodated by a network of intuitive, attractive, and consistent infrastructure. Just as more highways lead to more cars, developing bicycle infrastructure is the key to getting more residents to cycle. The old excuses for not embracing cycling, such as climate, culture, and topography, are no longer considered valid in cities around the world. While techno-utopianism

promises a future in which driverless vehicles and electric unicycles are poised to save humanity, the bicycle is right here, staring us in the face. Both simple and efficient, the bicycle is perfectly suited to address the many issues brought on by decades of automobile-centric urban traffic-planning. Cities around the world are beginning to plan for bicycle infrastructure that is intuitive, attractive, and consistent. The existing presence of such infrastructure proves that cycling is no longer reserved for middle-class men in lycra or hipster messengers, but for everyday people, yawning their way through their morning commute.

— by James Thoem
for Copenhagenize Design Co.

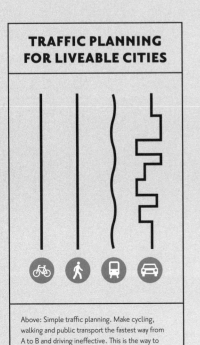

TRAFFIC PLANNING FOR LIVEABLE CITIES

Above: Simple traffic planning. Make cycling, walking and public transport the fastest way from A to B and driving ineffective. This is the way to change the mobility paradigm for the better.

TWO-Wheeled ARCHITECTURE

Traditionally, bike frames have been made of steel, and more recently, aluminum and carbon fiber. The most exotic frames, however, are titanium, and Berlin's **Wheeldan** *makes some of the world's finest.*

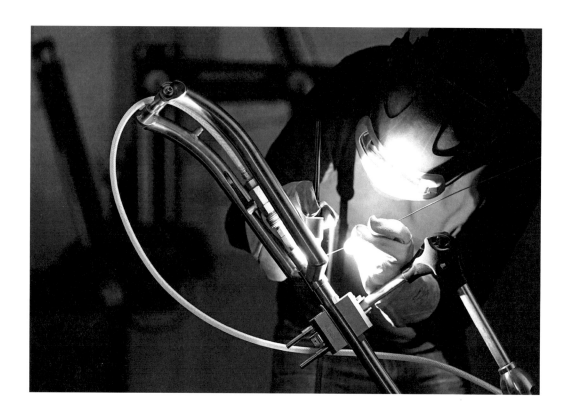

"Well done" is Daniel Pleikies mantra, a phrase that underlies the Wheeldan workshop. Daniel was a practicing architect who transformed his talent for creating spaces for humans into building two-wheeled human-powered vehicles. There are several parallels between the two disciplines: they're both governed by environment, ergonomics, and engineering, and they're both reliant on creative solutions to problems. Ideally, when executed well, both improve the lives of those who interact with them.

Pleikies eschewed his previous career path in 2011 after a decade in the industry, spurred by the birth of

– Below: **Wanderlust**—Wheeldans interpretation of a contemporary ultralightweight randonneur bike. 18.5 lbs (8.4 kg) complete with pedals, fenders, racks and dynamo system.

TITANIUM

is a robust material. Rustproof and weatherproof, lightweight but strong, titanium has many qualities that make it **SUPERIOR** to— and more expensive than—steel or aluminum.

– *Left:* **Doctors bike**, low maintenance
bike in everyday use of a doctor who visits
his clients by bicycle.
– *Top right:* The best of two worlds,
classic french porteur and German MTB-Tech.
– *Bottom:* Integrated titanium racks
with internal wire routing.

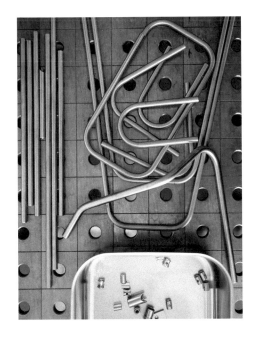

his son. The quest was for more time to raise his two children, who are now both becoming the beneficiaries of their father's new trade. One of the first projects in Pleikies's portfolio was a balance bike for his son, built entirely from titanium, handlebars included. He has since created machines ranging from tandems and super-commuters to elaborate randonneurs and mountain bikes. Titanium is, by nature, a desirable material that's completely rust proof and resilient to the weather. It's lighter, stronger, and rarer than steel and aluminum, but more expensive as well, and extremely unforgiving. Connecting two tubes together requires an experienced welding technique and a very steady hand. The workshop and materials must be clinically clean to ensure a

"My motivation is to produce an INDIVIDUAL, DURABLE, ELEGANT and technically meaningful vehicle."

– *Top left*: Super light 11 lbs (5 kg) kids bike for Daniel Pleikies' son.
– *Left*: Mini cargo bike for urban use with integrated child seat.

Travel tandem **Double Happiness** for father and son. The front is inspired by an old tandem front from 1910–1920.

WHEELDAN

– *Top Left*: French classic inspired randonneur with contemporary German technology, Rohloff plus Supernova dynamo lighting. Made for the "Rinko" travel system—wheels and fenders can easily be detached and the bike stored in a compact travelbag.
– *Top right*: Randonneur stem with own CNC machined clamp mechanism adds stack height for comfort. Position on long trips with integrated bell mount.

strong join which, for bicycle frames, is understandably crucial. Given his architectural background, the appeal for Pleikies was clear.

These days, his frames are highly sought after by both European and international customers, fetching prices indicative of the skill required to build them. There is an art to Pleikies's work with the silver-gray metal, and most of his completed frames leave the workshop in a raw unpainted state. Their matte brushed finish lends them a sculptural air, like a modernist concrete building with a few contrasting details.

Pleikies doesn't stop at the bike's frame and fork. He constructs the intricate baggage racks, which are specifically designed around the front dynamo hub wiring and headlights. In the case of his elaborate long-distance randonneur bikes, he'll fabricate the stem and pump mounts, and ensure the radius of the fender matches that of the tire. The brake lights are integrated, with every brake and derailleur cable considered—one should expect nothing less from an architect turned frame builder. <

Like a sleek MODERNIST building, the brushed matte finish lends the frame a sculptural air.

HUGE DESIGN
– EVO Urban Utility

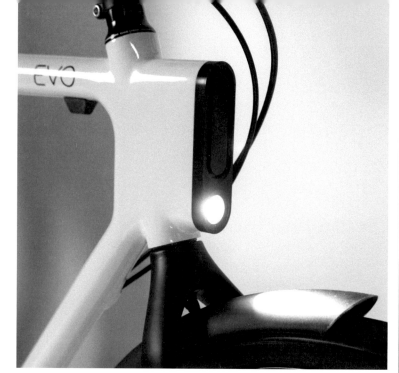

The hybrid EVO Urban Utility bike by Huge Design leverages a modular accessory platform for ultimate flexibility. By blending the utility of a city bike with the robust geometry of a mountain bike, the EVO works well in a wide variety of environments, such as the rough terrain found outside the design team's San Francisco base, and a wide range of activities, including urban commuting. The bike's innovative platform includes front and rear quick-connect mounts, enabling users to mix and match cargo accessories, which are usually permanently attached. Also included are integrated lights and an integrated lock for security. <

UNO
60 Lb CAPACITY
1 BAG or 1x 12 PACK CANS

– *Top:* After endless sketching, the final frame design becomes a reality. Still a handmade one-off, the mud guards are almost invisible and disc brakes come standard.
– *Left:* Rack capacity equals one bag or a pack of twelve cans.

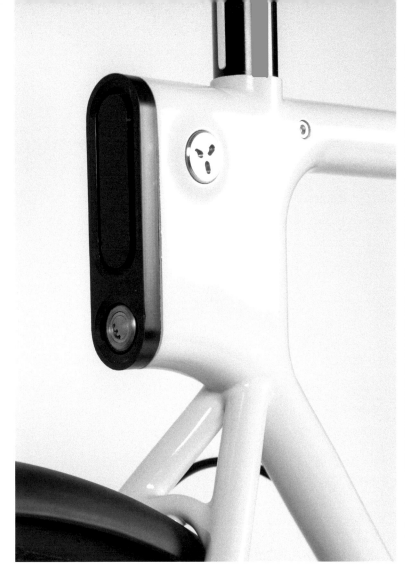

– *Top:* An integrated lock hidden in the frame comes standard on every frame.
– *Bottom:* The modular system accommodates everything from bicycle bags to a child seat. Two different racks are available in different sizes.

HUGE DESIGN—*EVO Urban Utility*

STRINGBIKE
– A line

The people behind Stringbike started with a blank slate to create a completely new biking experience. Their system does away with the shaft, chain, and belt drive for a clean, quiet, and joyful ride. It transfers pushing power from the legs into a pulling motion, through swinging arms and two double high-density polyethylene strings. It then transfers that power to the back wheel, where the rear hub converts it into circular movement. The rider can select from 19 gears by moving the rope wheels up and down, and can adjust each gear for all types of riding situations, while the kickback motion of the system pushes the bike forward with ease, even when pedaling backwards. The strings can be changed in two minutes without using stools, and can be washed when dusty. <

– *Opposite left*: Missing a chain? Nope! **Brikbikes** can be ordered with a shaft drive. What has been used on motorcycles for decades works just as great on a bicycle. Clean, reliable, quiet acceleration.
– *Opposite bottom right*: Different kinds of lights can be ordered by the customer. LED ended the age of low batterys and candlelike lighting.

BRIKBIKES
– *Brikbike by Anna*

The Brikbike by Anna is a collaboration between Dutch fashion house Anna van Toor and bicycle company Brikbikes. The stylish and practical design features the century-old shaft drive system, which is reliable, clean, and quiet. Different options are available, according to each customer's personal taste, for features such as lighting, child seats, handlebars, kickstands, and saddles. An AXA Solid lock comes as a standard feature on every model; and the entire RAL color range is available. The Anna is the bike for the modern Dutch woman. <

CANYON BICYCLES
– Commuter 8.0

– *Bottom:* The integrated steering head is one of **Canyon's** signature design features. All bikes are custom made by hand in a modern German factory.

The Commuter 8.0 by Canyon Bicycles is one of the most innovative bikes on the market. Designer **Lutz Scheffer**'s unique cockpit profile gives riders a fresh and unusual experience. Combining iconic aesthetics with exceptional functionality, Scheffer's bike has clean lines and fully integrated wiring matched to bright hub, dynamo-driven LED lights, effective Hexlox theft protection, luggage-carrying capacity, and mudguards. Low-maintenance components include the Gates belt drive and Shimano Alfine 11-speed gear hub. The saddle stem has a cushioning effect, transforming the urban riding experience into a positive adventure rather than a chore. <

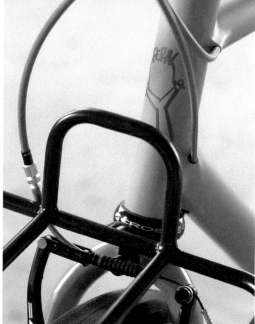

Joined forces from Berlin Lichtenberg.
Fern Fahrräder and Gramm Tourpacking
are working on the same floor.
Gramm is the address to get finest
bespoke bicycle bags.

FERN X GRAMM
– Chuck

Whether crossing a harsh desert landscape or touring the lush Berlin countryside, the Chuck easily tackles any terrain with its ultralight 26-inch (54 mm) tires. Built as a collaboration between Gramm Tourpacking and Fern Fahrräder, the Chuck is a randonneur/MTB hybrid that offers a variety of options for carrying Gramm bike bags on a custom-made 23 lbs (10.5 kg) frame. It also comes standard with light dynamo straps, low-trail/race geometry, and a Columbus tube set. <

MOKUMONO
– Delta

Not wanting to participate in the European trend of manufacturing bicycles overseas, Mokumono decided to do things differently. Inspired by the endlessly innovative European car industry, Mokumono reinvented the way bicycle frames are produced, by making the process completely automated, thus eliminating the need to send work abroad. The design reflects the unique way in which it is produced: two flat sheets of aluminum are pressed into shape, and then laser-welded together to form a strong, lightweight frame. <

SCHINDELHAUER BIKES
– Ludwig XIV and Hektor

The team of designers and engineers at Schindelhauer Bikes have a passion for pairing innovation with sophisticated design. Combining timeless elegance with clever functionality, they believe the future of bicycles is no noise, no grease, and low-maintenance belt drives.

The fully customizable Ludwig XIV (left) combines a 14-speed Rohloff Speedhub, a Formula R1 disc brake system, and a Gates Carbon Drive for a versatile, maintenance-free, and reliable ride. The Hektor frameset (right) is stiff and aggressive, yet nimble and dynamic, making it the perfect foundation upon which to tailor a custom racing bike, thanks to its LoPro geometry. It is the first track bike designed to maximize the potential of the Gates Carbon Drive. <

– *Top:* Ensuring that the drive belt works on a bike requires an ultra strong frame. **Schindelhauer** frames are made from 6061 aluminum that is tig-welded, heat treated, and then polished to improve strength.

KP CYCLERY
– The Bike Hanger 2.0

One of the more popular ideas when it comes to storage is to mount a beloved bicycle to the wall, and display it like a trophy. The Bike Hanger's mount comes with unique zig-zag screw slots to ensure that it stays securely fixed to the wall; and the adjustable wall offset can accommodate any bike. <

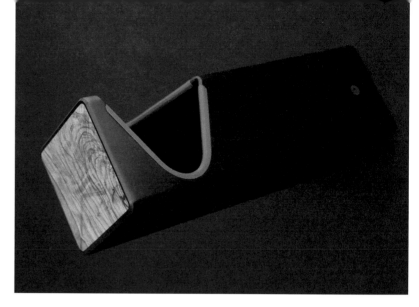

PARAX
– D-Rack

The Parax D-Rack is an interior bike rack for design-loving minimalists. Its aluminum body mounts directly to the wall and holds one bike, with a silicone-coated edge to prevent slipping and scratches. An optional wooden front panel provides a simple finishing touch to this practical but stylish piece. <

MARTIN FORET
– Heart

The Heart by Martin Foret, winner of the 2017 Red Dot design award, is a functional design object that provides sturdy and attractive indoor storage for the urban cyclist. Constructed from welded steel, and available in a black, red, or white powder-coated finish, the Heart guides a bike frame into place and evenly distributes its weight. <

MIKILI
– SLÎT

With its clever but simple design, the SLÎT by Mikili offers secure bike storage that can be folded up, and out of the way, when it is not needed. In addition to a felt overlay that prevents scratches to the frame, each rack comes with a felt strap that holds the front wheel securely in place. <

WOODSTICK BICYCLE GOODS
– Iceberg

Crafted from handpicked pieces of oak and birch, the Iceberg by Woodstick is a sculptural bike rack with a visually dynamic design. Needing only three standard screws, the Iceberg mounts easily to the wall, and comes with several finishing options to match any interior look. <

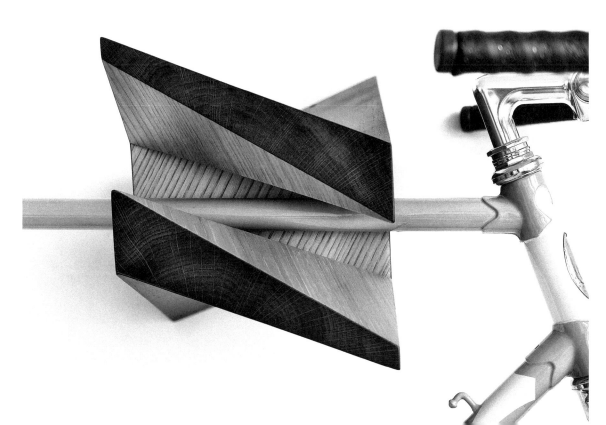

THOUSAND
– Epoch Collection

Not fans of wearing helmets themselves, the people behind Thousand's Epoch collection focused on a classic design with contemporary detailing, including copper hardware, matte colors, hydro-dipped printing, and vegan leather straps. Interior padding ensures a custom fit for every head. The helmet's Secret PopLock makes it possible to securely fasten it to a bike and comes with a Helmet Thief Guarantee. <

FEND
– Helmet

With its lightweight foldable design, the FEND helmet fits easily into the back-pack of any urban cyclist. Streamlined vents ensure that it is breathable, while its minimal design is engineered for the ultimate in safety. <

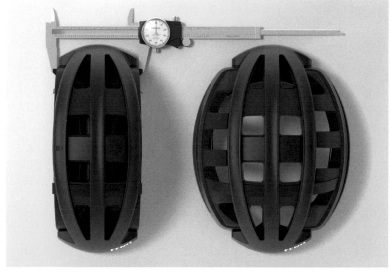

CLOSCA
– Helmet

More than just a bicycle helmet, the Closca provides safety, comfort, and exceptional portability to every cyclist who wears it. Its lightweight design offers a ventilation system and interchangeable visors, and it folds flat for easy storage; and it does all this while exceeding international safety certifications. <

MEAME
– Altair Biker Jacket,
Alpha Reflective
Tweed Blazer

Meame's collection of performance clothing for urban cyclists features outerwear that combines the newest fabric technology with classic styles. Their waterproof jackets for men and women include reflective safety features, as well as ventilation and temperature regulation. <

SHOWERS PASS
– Atlas Jacket

With its waterproof but breathable design, the Atlas Jacket is perfect for commuting around town or traveling around the world. Its MapREflect fabric features 11 well-known cycling cities, screen-printed in reflective ink, providing safety when on the road. <

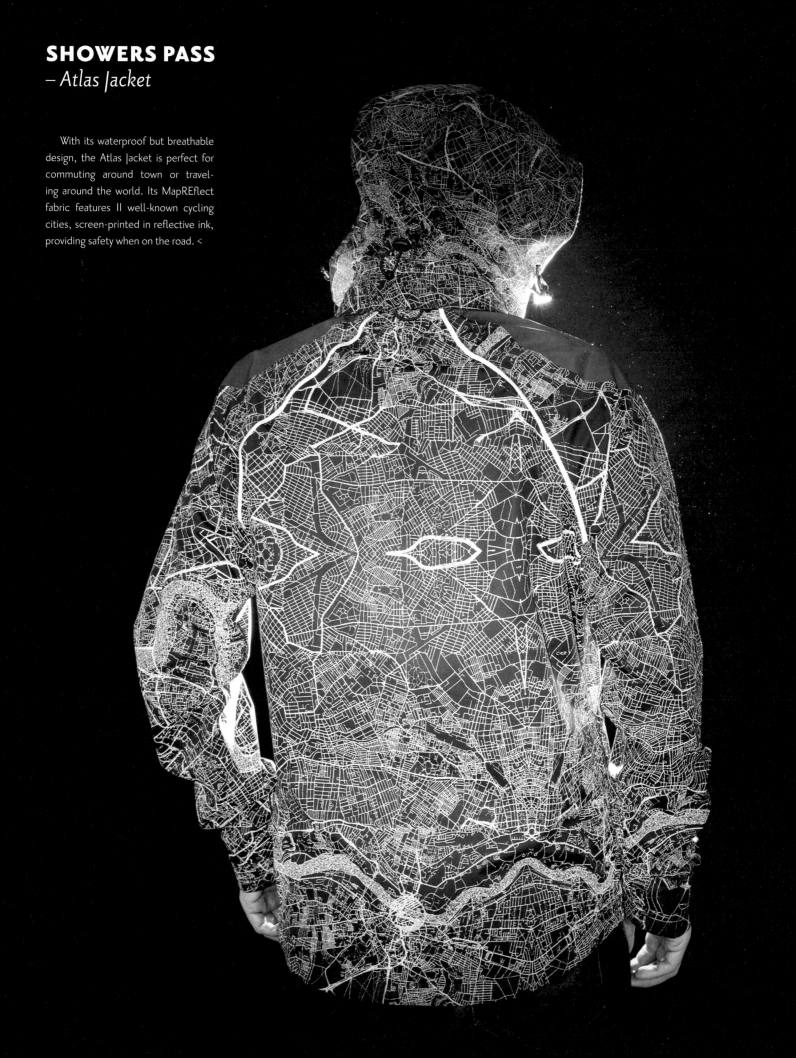

RAPHA
– Reflective Quarter Zip Knit and Pack Jacket in Dot Print

Weighing less than 0.22 lbs (0.1 kg), and able to fold into a diminutive package, the windproof and rainproof Pack Jacket is the perfect accessory for city cycling, and features an interpretation of the legendary "maillot à pois" dot pattern. For low light conditions, the Reflective Quarter Zip Knit is the perfect choice, combining antibacterial and odor-inhibiting Merino wool with a reflective yarn. <

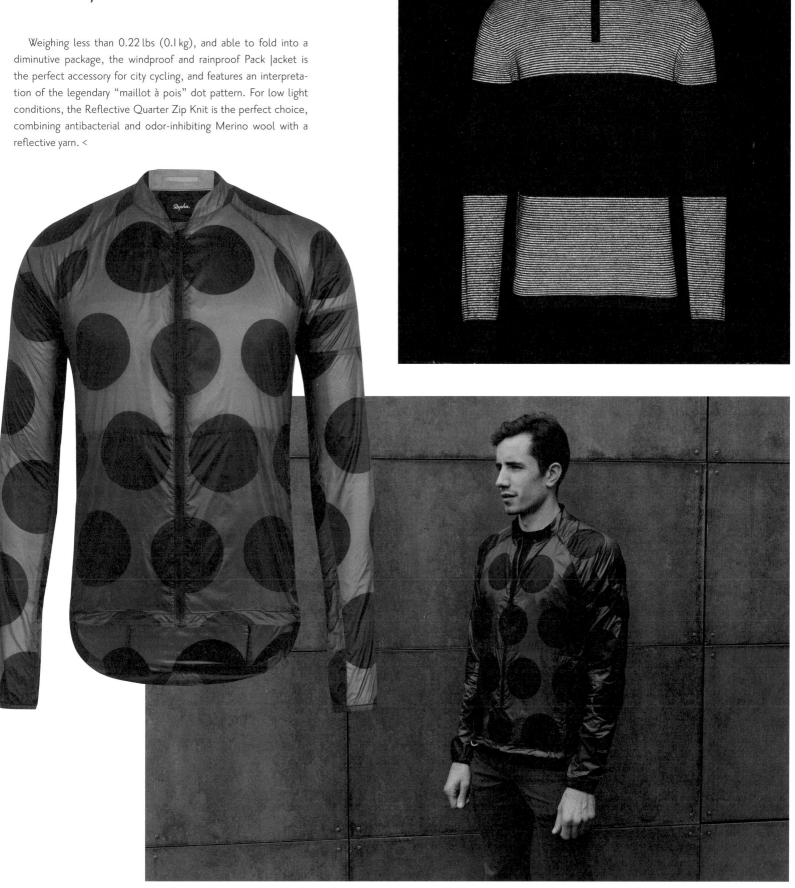

TERN
– Vizy Light

With its 360° pool of light, the Tern Vizy Light illuminates a cyclist's entire body and the ground around them, encouraging cars to maintain a wide berth. Its 60 lumens of brightness and its quick-release mounting system make it brighter than any other bicycle light, and easy to remove when needed. <

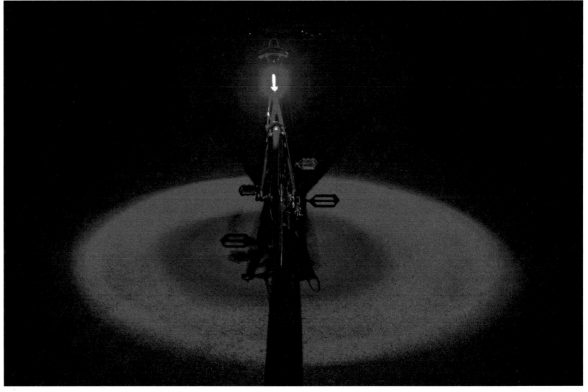

PRODUCTS—*Lights*

REVOLIGHTS
– Eclipse

The Revolights bike lighting system Eclipse features 360° visibility lighting for low light and night riding. The system, which automatically turns on when needed, features rechargeable batteries and smart brake lights. The Revolights app offers accurate ride tracking, battery status, and weather alerts. <

LUMOS
– Helmet

With integrated lights and turn signals, the Lumos Helmet is the first smart helmet of its kind. Its 48 front and back LED lights ensure safety in the darkest of conditions. When its wearer slows down, the helmet automatically switches all rear LEDs to bright red. Weatherproof and equipped with its own smartphone app, the Lumos has every need covered for the urban commuter. <

BLAZE
– Laserlight and Burner

The bike lights produced by Blaze combine technology with design to create a new experience for the urban cyclist. Blaze's products feature ultrabright LEDs, waterproof casing, laser technology, and long-lasting batteries for better visibility on the road. <

WACHSEN
— WK-001

The low profile WK-001 from Wachsen is a stylish bike lock that works well for cyclists taking quick breaks. Included with every lock is a pass case that holds the lock's key and ensures that it is always close at hand. Antique gold finishes and vegan leather make the lock coordinate easily with any wardrobe. <

PALOMAR
— Lochness

The bendable design of the Lochness is an unusual alternative to the traditional bike lock. Its flexibility means that it can easily fit around anything in the urban landscape to which a bike might need to be secured; and, unlike a u-lock, it molds to the bike frame to ensure a rattle-free ride. <

TIGR LOCK
– TiGr mini+

Attaching easily to any bike frame via the water bottle mount, the titanium u-lock "mini+" from TiGr is lightweight and unobtrusive when on the go, and ultrasecure when in use. Each lock provides a 7 × 4 inch locking area with a push button locking mechanism. <

TEX-LOCK
– tex-lock

Available in three sizes and four colors, the Tex-Lock is a strong, hightech-textile-based lock with a unique loop through system. The Tex-Lock's layered textile construction makes it as strong as any steel lock but with the added features of flexibility and a stylish look. <

VEL-OH
– Worker Bag, Blackpack

Made from British Millerain waxed cotton canvas, Vel-Oh backpacks keep their contents dry in almost any weather, and look good while doing so. From messenger bags to backpacks, each bag in the Vel-Oh line is designed to have more than one function, and is made for cyclists, by cyclists. <

LUMABAG
– Urban Traveller

All Lumabags are made by hand in Bremen, Germany by **Uwe Malte Arndt**, using recycled materials. The Urban Traveller is constructed with durable waxed cotton, making it perfect for the everyday urban cyclist. Easy clip-ons and a recycled bicycle tire support a stable mount. <

HILL & ELLIS
– Bradley Bike Bag

With its eye-catching yellow leather, the Bradley Bike Bag is a must-have piece for cyclists who want to make a statement. Special features include a central locking system, a waterproof bag jacket, and a leather shoulder strap. <

PEDALFACTORY
— The Sandwichbike

The award-winning Sandwichbike, designed by Netherlands-based Pedalfactory, takes its inspiration from the concept of flat packing. Instead of a welded frame, the Sandwichbike consists of two weather-coated frames of sustainably-harvested plywood. Bonded together by smart cylinders, the frames and components create a durable bike that fits into a small, flat package that can easily be sent by post. Everything needed for assembly is included in the box, giving customers the unique experience of being able to engage in the creation of their own bicycle. <

The Sandwichbike can be ordered with a wooden fork (as shown) or steel fork and comes with the option of a one or two-speed set up. A limited edition walnut veneer is also available.

GRAINWORKS WOOD ART
– AnalogOne.One

Woodworker **Mike Pecsok** doesn't stick to one type of project—he's crafted everything from rolling pins to custom cabinets. After a friend challenged him to build a bike out of wood, he created the AnalogOne.One out of mahogany, walnut, maple, and cherry. It features a frame made from 39 laminated pieces of wood and a chain stay and seat stay made with bent lamination. Though the objects he creates are aesthetically pleasing, his working philosophy honors function over form, and he takes his inspiration from the mechanical workings of equipment and infrastructure projects such as bridges. <

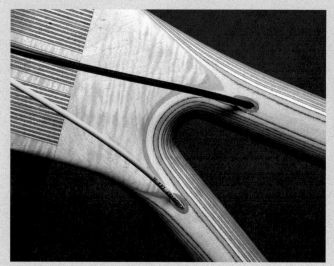

It's all in the details; excellence in craftsmanship, not just when building furniture. Top quality laminating and dovetail connections.

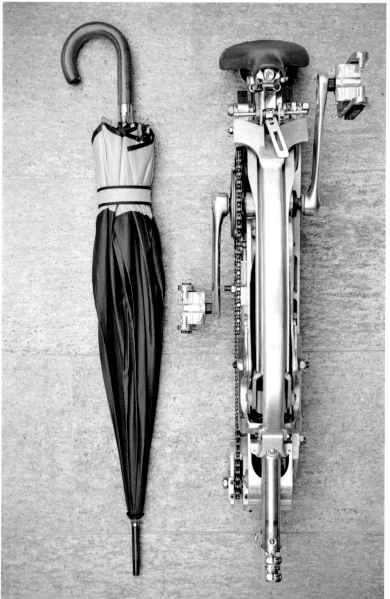

GIANLUCA SADA
– Sada Bike

Gianluca Sada's hubless Sada Bike needs only one movement to fold its frame into an object the size of an umbrella. Its tiny size makes it perfect for commuters who want the convenience of throwing their bike into a backpack or under a desk. Recognizing that small folding bikes hinder the rider when traversing long distances or varied terrains, Sada placed a high priority on maintaining a standard frame size for his folding design. Unlike most bicycles, which get their strength from tension in the spokes, the Sada Bike maintains its size and collapsibility by eliminating the spokes and relying instead on its rims for strength. <

DOPPELGÄNGER
– 260 Parceiro, 202X Giant Killing, 266 Master-piece

Folding bikes are gaining popularity, especially in urban environments, and Japanese-made Doppelgänger bicycles are part of this trend. With an affordable price point, 20-inch (50 cm) wheels, and features like a Shimano gear shifter, everyone is certain to find a Doppelgänger ("look-alike" in German) that fits their needs. The 260 Parceiro comes with a foldable diamond frame—a first—and is available in various retro color schemes. The 266 Master-piece and 202X Giant Killing models, with their stiff parallel twin frames, fit people between 5 feet (150 cm) and 6 feet (180 cm) in height, making the bikes attractive to families. <

– *Right bottom, Top Left:* **260 Larceiro**
– *Bottom left, Top right:* **202X Giant Killing**
– *Opposite Top left:* **266 Master-Piece**

MONTAGUE
– Paratrooper and Allston

For over 25 years, Cambridge, Massachusetts-based Montague has served as a world leader in full-size folding bikes. Focused on performance and ride quality, the company delivers road and mountain bikes that go where others cannot. First developed in the late 1990s, the rugged Paratrooper allows airborne soldiers to drop out of airplanes and into combat with a bike. The virtually maintenance-free Allston is perfect for touring or commuting; it folds in seconds for travel or storage, and requires no lubrication. <

– *Right:* The **Moulton NS Marathon** with advanced Flexitor® front suspension, Hydrolastic® rear suspension and a lighter polished stainless steel frame.
– *Left:* The **Moulton NS Double Pylon** comes with 22 gears Campagnolo Super Record and a Moulton wishbone Q Stem. Stainless stell pylons replace head and seat tubes.

MOULTON BICYCLE COMPANY
– NS Double Pylon & NS Marathon

In the late 1950s, **Dr. Alex Moulton** set out to completely redesign the bicycle. His disregard of convention freed him from any expectation of what a bicycle should look like and ultimately led him to an innovative design. Released in 1962, the original Moulton Bicycle was an immediate success. The company continues to endure today, with some of its original employees still in-house. With significant advancements in bicycle design, Moulton bikes feature high-end welding, variable suspension options, and small but strong wheels to allow more responsive steering and faster acceleration. Moultons have a huge fan-base in crowded cities like Tokyo. <

CASTRO BIKES
– Castro MI

Created by Barcelona-based designers **Antonio Castro** and **Ana Zubelzu**, the Castro MI folding bike features a highly flexible design, taking up so little space that it can be stored almost anywhere. With just two quick movements—a turn of the handlebar and a pull on the aluminum Ezy MSK removable pedals—the bike folds flat into a 9-inch (23 cm) package. Its one-size-fits-all AISI 304 electropolished stainless steel single frame adjusts to a variety of positions, while the adjustable seat also allows for a 2.75-inch (7 cm) horizontal variation. The bike is available with an automatic 2-speed or 3-speed coaster brake, and a 2.75-inch (7 cm) drum brake in the rear hub. <

HELIX
– Helix Folding Bike

Made from durable lightweight titanium, the Helix folds down to the size of its wheels with a patent-pending, side-by-side design. When folded, it pushes effortlessly and can be parked with an integrated stand, and locked with a spring-loaded mechanism that passes through the fork and steerer tubes for extra security. Despite its small size and light weight, the Helix is durable enough to ride every day, and accommodates a range of accessories, including mud guards, racks, and lights. Interchangeable dropouts make it easy to switch between drivetrain options. <

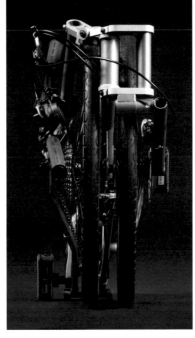

DEAR SUSAN
– Talldax

U. K.-based one-man-company Dear Susan sells joy in the form of bicycles. Designer **Petor Georgallou** first built his Talldax frame at The Bicycle Academy in Frome, Somerset. Made from a mix of Columbus and t45 tubes, the height keeps feet dry; and the unique design provides enough space to transport camping or picnic equipment. The bike features a removable Brompton rack, lights, and mudguards, and offers, despite its weird form, everything a daily commuter bike has. The unusual look of the bike piques the interest of all who see it, and has resulted in Georgallou, while cycling around Europe, being invited into the homes of strangers, intrigued by his mode of transportation. <

Each Veloheld model can be ordered in any RAL color combination.
Left: The **Veloheld.Lane Pizza** comes with an ordered front rack.

VELOHELD
— Veloheld.Lane

Each bike at Dresden-based Veloheld is handmade, with a special focus on sustainable materials. Clients are also given a custom choice of color combinations and parts, making every bike that leaves the workshop unique. Over the years, Veloheld has produced everything from city bikes to touring, racing, and fat bikes. The Veloheld. Lane Pizza, with a front rack, and the Lane in olive green (right) both come with a carbon belt and 11-gear Shimano Alfine, as well as modern LED lights. <

– *Top:* Handmade mixed
metal head badge by
Jen Green featuring a capybara.
– *Left:* Disc brake cables
run through the fork leg.

70

GALLUS CYCLES
– Frank's Adventure Bike

Jeremy Shlachter, the man behind Gallus Cycles started off by merging classic randonneur characteristics with throwback MTB style for a passionate bicycle lover named Frank. The frame is made from a mix of Columbus Zona and Cromor tubes joined by bi-laminate construction. The long partslist starts off with 650b × 2.2 inch tires, disc brakes, Brooks Cambium saddle and 9-speed Dura-Ace shifters. Cutlass Velo built the Pacenti rims with Sapim spokes along with a White Industries hub in the rear and Schmidt Son28 dynamo hub at the front. A custom modular touring rack and detachable low riders for panniers are perfect for carrying camping gear. The colour is Porsche Leaf Green with darker green lettering matching the racks. <

DIAMANT
– 133

Diamant founders **Friedrich** and **Wilhelm Nevoigt** built their first bicycle in 1895, in the small village of Reichenbach, near Chemnitz, Germany. By 1898, they had invented the bicycle chain as we know it today. After Trek bought the company, they began the tradition of offering an annual jubilee model. The limited edition 133 celebrates the company's 133rd anniversary, and uses the classic diamond head over handlebar logo that debuted in 1911. Other features include mechanic Promax disc brakes, hub dynamo, LED lights, low-maintenance Shimano Alfine 8-speed hubs, a Brooks saddle and bag, and a 32 lbs (14.6 kg) steel frame and fork that come with a 40-year guarantee. <

MÖVE BIKES
– franklin

Unable to find a bike that met their standards, the team at Möve Bikes built their own ride, the Möve franklin, which sports a patented Cyfly drive and a special frame. The innovative drive system of the cyfly, whose redesigned foot pedal is disconnected from the axel, increases torque by an impressive 33%. Möve Cyfly involves 100 individual parts that work together. This includes precision-milled and calibrated gear wheels made from high-performance steel, and a custom-made low-friction rotary shaft seal. On a side note, the industry ball bearings have a long-life grease guarantee, which is perfect for maintenance-shy users. <

74

DONHOU BICYCLES
– Town Bike

Tom Donhou's epiphany, that he needed to make his own bicycles, came to him during a cycling trip across the Gobi Desert. Fast-forward to the present, and Donhou runs an award-winning East London workshop known for producing some of the world's finest steel bicycles. His modern Town Bike is an understated but refined take on a classic, built entirely with Reynolds 953 stainless steel. The bike runs fixed with disc brakes that add the guaranteed stopping power needed in unpredictable London traffic. Finishing details include a beautifully-crafted front-rack, a braze-on bell mount, a steering lock with a key, and a mandatory Brooks saddle. <

– *Left*: The manual disc brake setup.
– *Top*: Smooth frame lines.

SPEEDVAGEN
– Urban Racer

Portland-based Speedvagen is a collaborative work-shop of master fabricators, mechanics, and craftspeople, all working together to create the best bicycles. Their Urban Racer is a minimalist bike that comes in three stock sizes, with two color options: matte army green or hot pink. The frame is made from extra strong steel and weighs in at just 13 lbs (6 kg). A coaster brake and a 2-speed internal SRAM hub that shifts automatically at 10 mph (16 km/h) support the minimal look. The bike can also be upgraded with a bar/stem combo, integrated lighting, and a front rack and bag. <

URWAHN
– Stadtfuchs

Driven by a mission to take urban mobility to a whole new level, Urwahn bikes are designed to overcome the challenges of urban commuting. During the development process, an emphasis was placed on exceptional user experience, by focusing on function, performance, and safety, as well as aesthetics. The result is an unusual form-fitting frame design that can absorb minor shocks from the rear wheel, creating a completely new riding experience. The bike's integrated lights and stem, GPS tracker, built-in dynamo in the front wheel hub, disc brakes, and belt drive set the standard for modern cycles. Stadtfuchs is expected to be production-ready in early 2018. <

– Top: The most striking characteristic of the **Stadtfuchs** (German for city fox) is the curved frame with minimal damping function.

THE MAN behind Budnitz BICYCLES

Ready to go beyond his worldwide cult toy brand, Kidrobot, American entrepreneur **Paul Budnitz** *ventured into the boutique bicycle market. Will urban cycling ever be the same?*

– *Left:* Paul Budnitz, the man behind many ideas.
– *Right:* **Model No. I** with a titanium frame and grease-free belt drive.

If you have only heard of Paul Budnitz as a fan of his bikes or collectable toys, you only know a fraction of the story behind this creative, innovative, and intriguing man. He's founded over a dozen companies and established ad-free social media platforms, made films and written books, delivered lectures on art, entrepreneurship, and creativity, and has 13 designs in the permanent collection of New York's Museum of Modern Art. He's also been riding bikes his whole life.

Budnitz initially studied physics at Yale, but switched to an arts degree, halfway through, focusing on photography, sculpture, and film. His first enterprise

BUDNITZ BICYCLES

– *Top right:* **Model No. 1** with a carbon fork and short wheel base, ideal for speedy commuting. Crafted from rust free 3AL 2.5V titanium allow that is custom drawn, butted, and tig welded.

was distributing silk-screened shirts to museum stores around the world, which extended into procuring and selling vintage Levis and sneakers to collectors. All the while, he was working on scores for his films recorded on modified MiniDisc players, which evolved into a $10,000,000 (€8,140,000) business, run out of a garage on software he had written himself.

He maintains that the reason for his success lies in following what he loves and is passionate about, an ethos that inspired him to establish Budnitz Bicycles in 2010. The mission statement was to create bikes that were at the utmost pinnacle of quality and rideability. Only a few hundred bikes are produced each year, constructed completely from titanium—including the

"The BUSINESS MODEL is one quite unlike any others in the industry: STAY SMALL."

– Top right: Available options include mud guards, bicycle bags, titanium bottle holder, LED lights, and other premium parts.

forks—and with only the highest caliber components. The business model centers around staying small. A more personal relationship is established with customers in this way, allowing for tailored bike customization. Visitors are warmly welcomed to Budnitz's studio, located in Burlington, Vermont. Here they can browse the range and watch their assembly. There are currently six models on offer, including two electric versions. All of the bikes, in each model, have a very recognizable aesthetic, with gracefully sweeping tubes and a pared-back look that lacks any garish logos or graphics. Even the model names are stylishly devoid

He maintains that the reason for his SUCCESS lies in following what he loves and is passionate about.

of embellishments. There's the Alpha, No.1, No.3, Model Ø, Model E, and bella E. Each model delivers at the height of performance. Built from aerospace grade titanium (with alternative 4130 Chromoly seamless steel tube options), with a cantilever frame design, carbon belt drive, and internal geared hubs, so there's no chance of greasy residue leaving marks on your legs. Budnitz Bicycles have been touted as the Aston Martin of bikes, and it's not hard to see why. <

– *Left:* The **Bella E** has a Zehus Bike+ 250 W motor and a self-charging 30V L-ion 160 Wh battery enclosed in an elegant aluminum rear hub. It reaches a maximum speed of 15 mph (24 km/h) and has a battery range of 20 to 100 miles (32 to 161 km).

The Origins and Rennaissance of the CARGO BIKE

When searching for the origins of the first cargo bike, several sources will lead you to England, in the year 1877, where a gentleman named James Starley drew three carrier designs for transportation of goods and people. At that time, the cargo bike was very heavy, had just one gear, and could only carry small loads; the chain, as we know it today, had not been invented yet. Over time, frame tubes, the chain, and smaller wheels made the riding experience more enjoyable. In the twentieth century—the Golden Age of the cargo bike—an unknown English man got the idea of positioning a large box in front of the driver, right above a horizontal front axle, which worked as a complete steering unit. Thus, the first classical cargo bike (still known as carrier) was born. As frames became more rigid, bikes could handle larger loads, and eventually the maximum load was limited only by the rider's physical condition. With these improvements, the bike became suitable for the hard work faced by craftsmen, postmen, and garbage collectors. After the Second World War, Western cities saw a rapid shift to motorized delivery

LARRY VS. HARRY—BULLITT BLUEBIRD

vehicles and cargo bikes started to disappear with the exception of a few pockets in the Netherlands, where the large wooden bakfiets (traditional heavy tricycles with a large heavy cargo bed at the front) were still in use. Bakfiets literally means "box bike," but the term is now used for three-wheelers, as well as for two-wheeled, cargo-type bikes. In the mid-1980s, the Danes began to produce three-wheelers in the freetown of Christiania. The Christiania bike was born, and became a huge hit amongst families, and was also adopted as a mode of transport for the postal service;

and the rennaissance of the Cargo bike had begun. By the year 2,000, Copenhagen had more than 10,000 on the streets, and both Danish and Dutch manufacturers started exporting worldwide. If the Christiania bike was the poster child of a car-free life, the "Bullitt," by Larry vs. Harry, took the messengers' world by storm: bike riders dropped their fixies and started riding the fastest, sexiest cargo bike ever designed. Because of the increased political attention given to climate change and air quality over the last three years, the cargo bike is increasingly mentioned as a twenty-first century mobility solution.

Why get a cargo bike?

Child transportation is one of the main reasons people purchase a cargo bike, so the cargo bike becomes an obvious choice for young families. This has considerable social and environmental impacts, because a family with a cargo bike has no need for a car. This reduces the amount of cars on the road, as well as the amount of cars fighting for parking spaces. The shift in the mindset of society is still in progress, since the automotive industry has left such a profound mark on everyday life in industrial nations. A cargo bike is not a hippy dream, but rather, a worthy and already accessible investment, unlike the future of the autonomous car industry, which is still a long way off reaching our streets. For professionals, such as tradesmen and window-cleaners, the costs of transportation are reduced massively if a cargo bike is used. It saves on fuel, taxes, insurance, and maintenance, and allows for a more spontanious and efficient change of operational radius, all of which adds up to a very attractive business transportation tool in inner city operations.

How to choose your cargo bike

In the past 20 years, we have seen a considerable increase in the quality of cargo bikes as well as a greater variety of makes and models available on the market. The key decision for buyers is this: three wheels or two? The singletrack cargo bikes are used mostly for quick urban deliveries. They have a large basket/box at the front, which is accommodated by a small front wheel or an elongated platform between the steering column and front wheel. The Long|ohn is used as a family bike, most notably in the Netherlands, Germany, Denmark, and France. Urban Arrow in the Netherlands is stretching the limits of what can be carried in front of the rider. In North America, the Long tail, a long rear rack or platform (see Yuba bikes page: 100–101) is popular as a personal cargo bike. Other singletrack frame designs include: Carrier Cycle, Butchers Bike, Frontloader, Long Diamond, singletrailer, Luggage Rack, and Lowtail. Most three-wheelers use the Centerpivot, which gives good maneuverability, but is less stable than the Ackermann system, where the wheels move independently of the cargobox (HNF Heisenberg). Rearsteer Trikes are a rare sight. Cyclelogistics operators use large tricycles able to carry 551 lbs (250 kg); the cargobox is located behind the rider, and is also known as a Delta Trike. Some models have four wheels with the rider

The Christiania bike with center pivot steering.

in a sitting position (Cargoquad). The best choices will depend on the rider's needs and environment: for instance, in a busy city with little provision for safe cycling, a tricycle is much safer than a two-wheeler. Similarly, if you live in a hilly rural setting, you can't go wrong with an electric two-wheeler, whose power, quality, and action radius has increased dramatically, thanks to automotive supply companies like Bosch and Brose. A good piece of advice might be, "Listen to the children too!" They may be one of the main reasons why you are buying the cargo bike and their perspective may be different from yours: while you are comparing gears or the design of the seats, they may prefer the bike which is easiest to get on and off by themselves.

The advent of central motors, located near the cranks, which

TERN BICYCLES—GSD ⟶ p. 102

URBAN ARROW—FAMILY ⟶ p. 104

EXPERT ESSAY—*Cargo Bikes*

CARGO BIKE ARCHETYPES

Singletrack cargo bikes

| Carrier Cycle | Butchers Bike | Frontloader | Long Diamont | Long John | Luggage Rack | Longtail | Lowtail |

Multitrack cargo bikes

| Centerpivot | Ackermann | Rearstear Trike | Trailer | Deltatrailer | Delta Trike | Cargoquad |

Cargobike Archetypes by Eric Poscher from Noun Project. www.thenounproject.com

enable a higher torque than rear hub motors, is particularly beneficial for cargo bikes, because the priority is shifting the weight rather than speed. We will therefore see cargo bikes become appealing in more areas and to a wider demographic: for example, an electric cargo bike becomes a very practical alternative to the mobility scooter for many elderly people.

Cargo bike hire for car-free living

Cargo bike prices (typically from $2,500 (€2,000) to $4,900 (€4,000), the latter for electric

As a work tool, the cargo bike is being recognised as a very effective tool.

assist models) may put off certain type of buyers, especially those who don't have a daily need for them. A solution which is becoming popular in European cities is the cargo bike public hire. One of the most successful initiatives uses a model which is different from the standard cycle public hire. The cargo bikes are hosted by local small

businesses who facilitate the pick-up and drop-off by local residents. The Carvelo2Go scheme now operates in more than 20 Swiss towns and cities, and has 140+ electric cargo bikes available. Do you need to pick up pots of paints for your home decoration or do you want to take your friend with her suitcases to the station? Easy, book a cargo bike

from your local shop and you can accomplish your task with ease and fun. The success of Carvelo2Go is spreading to other cities: Köln has recently started a similar scheme, and the City of London is conducting a feasibility study.

Cycle logistics—Back to business

Cargo bikes have the potential not just to shift the way we shop and get groceries, but also to take over the transport of goods usually covered by vans or trucks in city centers in the long run. All the major courier companies like DHL are introducing

FRANCES CYCLES—MIXTEHAUL ⟶ p. 118

FLEXIMODAL

Top: **Muli** cargo bike in Hamburg.
Above: Butchers & Bicycles **MKI-E.**
Right: The **PEK** from the Danish company
Biomega is a compact cargo bike.

BIOMEGA—PEK ⟶ p. II4

cargo bikes in their urban delivery fleets, and many cycle logistics companies have emerged. The last-mile model is being redrawn with many cities making available storage areas for micro-consolidation hubs, where parcels are shifted to small electric vehicles and cargo bikes. One feature that is helping this trend is the introduction of moveable containers that can be easily lowered into cargo bikes, making the transfer between vehicles more efficient. Velove in Sweden and Radkutsche in Germany are both developing this concept. As people see more and more cargo bikes being used for deliveries, the overall perception will shift, again as the smart choice for urban mobility. As a work tool, the cargo bike is being recognised as a very effective tool both by large businesses and young entrepreneurs.

Yes we can!

The Danish Cycling Pioneers (Larry vs. Harry), the designers of the Bullitt (a sleek modern version of the traditional Long|ohn) say: "We wanted to make it sexy." There were other similar bikes at the time, but something in the design of the Bullitt caught the excitement of its target audience. Similarly, cargo bike promotion needs to look at deep human motivators and find the triggers that will make people get excited about owning and using a cargo bike. When people feel that their vehicle, parked outside or in the garage, tells a lot about who they are, the cargo bike industry needs to create an image that cargo-bike riders are smart and modern, and represent future mobility. With sportier cargo bikes, better motors, and bigger batteries, people are starting to entertain long distance trips on a cargo bike. Tent and bags can be carried with greater comfort than cramped on a standard bike. The cargo bike gets a new role in the outdoor community. Compact cargo bikes like the "Muli" are so light you can carry them on the train, which widens widening the field of action. Indeed, we see a widespread shift towards the view that using a car in the city is wasteful and anti-social (i.e. not smart). Urban planners need to create streets where motorized vehicles don't undermine the joy of riding a cargo bike; in other words, the image of car-free cities needs to become mainstream in urban design and the society. The cargo bike is here—it is all about you now. Let's ride!

— *by Andrea Casalotti*

EXPERT ESSAY—*Cargo Bikes*

– *Top:* The **Omnium Cargo** comes with nylon webbing.
– *Below:* A rack extender is available for the **Omnium Mini-Max**.
– *Bottom:* The **Omnium Mini** comes with the shortest wheel base.

OMNIUM
– Cargo, Mini-Max, Mini

The Copenhagen-based workshop Omnium offers various cargo bike models with different wheelbase options and components. The work of designers **Jody Barton, Jimmi Bargisen,** and team, bike options include the Omnium Mini, the Omnium Cargo, and the Omnium Mini-Max, as well as a kids' model. All bikes have cargo nylon webbing in common, which can hold the weight of an adult and adapt to different kinds of cargo, as well as child seats. The latest addition to the company's range is the Omnium Cargo Electric, which features an integrated Shimano STEPS 8,000 power unit. On the top end stands the Omnium Ti, a custom-built titanium version of the regular Cargo with a frame weight of only 7.7 lbs (3.5 kg). <

– *Left:* The **Yuba Sweet Curry**.
– *Right:* The **Yuba Mundo**. Longtail cargo bikes are especially beloved in the United States.
– *Bottom left:* The **Yuba Supermarché** with electrical support is the company's latest model.
– *Bottom middle and bottom right:* The **Yuba Spicy Curry** offers electric support as well as different tail options.

YUBA BIKES
– *Sweet Curry, Supermarché, Spicy Curry, Mundo*

Yuba founder **Ben Sarrazin** grew up on two wheels in Strasbourg, France. While traveling as an adult, he witnessed everything from merchants in East Africa transporting their goods on two wheels, to people in Latin America choosing bikes over trucks, to better traverse dirt roads. The lesson he learned: for not much money, bikes can make lives better in rural areas, as well as in the city. Eventually Sarrazin founded Yuba Bikes, named after the California river where he loves to kayak and connect with the natural world. At Yuba, he makes a wide range of cargo bikes that are stable and safe, and reflect his family's love of being outdoors and living a healthy lifestyle. <

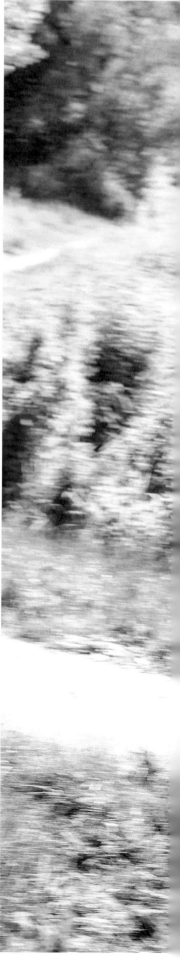

TERN BICYCLES
– GSD

Even though it's just 71 inches (180 cm) long, the GSD by Taiwan-based Tern Bicycles can carry two kids and a week's worth of groceries—or almost 400 lbs (180 kg) of cargo. Its small size, which is comparable to that of a standard e-bike, also makes it easy to store. The folding technology developed by Tern is the best in its class, turning this cargo bike into a package so small it can fit in the back of an average-sized car. Best of all, because it can adjust to fit riders ranging in height from 5–6 feet (150–180 cm) tall, both adults and kids can use it. <

URBAN ARROW
— Family

Dutch company Urban Arrow is making all cities greener and quieter with their range of electric cargo bikes that quickly move people and goods through city streets. The commercial benefits of the Shorty Flatbed include low costs per mile and high-speed travel that doesn't require a scooter license. For those looking to carry a lot of cargo while bypassing traffic jams, the Cargo L is a speedy and efficient ride. At home, look no further than Urban Arrow's Family line, comfortably transporting kids with a light aluminum frame that offers customizable seat options. <

BUTCHERS & BICYCLES
— MKI-E

Fast, safe, and super easy to ride, the MKI-E is an e-cargo bike that combines the comfort of an automobile with the freedom of a bike. Because the MKI-E leans into every turn, it is stable enough to ride with kids or on uneven roads. Climbing hills or riding long distances with children and groceries onboard is effortless, thanks to an integrated and powerful Bosch Performance CX motor. Voted Best Cargo Bike at Cyclingworld Düsseldorf in 2017, the MKI-E is a proven favorite and an everyday roller coaster ride for the little ones in the box. <

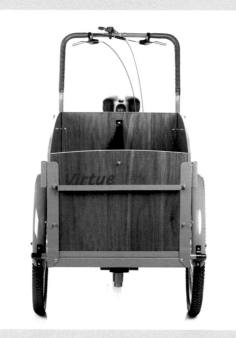

VIRTUE CYCLES
– Schoolbus+ and Gondoliere+

Based in San Diego, California, Virtue Cycles was founded in 2009 to promote practical and fun transportation solutions for a healthy lifestyle. When it comes to cycling with small children, many parents either strap their kids into a bike seat or put them in a trailer, but neither solution is stable or safe. Not only do the sturdy wooden boxes of the Schoolbus+ and Gondoliere+ make cycling with kids safer, they allow the whole family to interact while riding. Li-ion battery-powered electric assist, featured on both models, comes in handy when the kids, pets, and groceries get heavy. <

CARGO BIKE MONKEYS
– Radlader and eTurbolader

Based in Münster, Germany, Cargo Bike Monkeys builds lightweight but heavy-duty cargo bikes for city dwellers. The spaceframe for both models is handmade in Athens, Greece, and weighs 40 lbs (18 kg). Featuring an aluminum fork, internal cable steering, and multiple gear options, it is ready to carry any load up to 400 lbs (180 kg).

The smaller model, the eTurbolader (eLader Pendix), has a shorter wheel-base and comes with an additional noise-less electric motor with three riding modes, which are easy to select with the press of a button. Its interchangeable Pendix battery packs offer ranges from 65 miles (105 km) to 199 miles (320 km). <

RIESE & MÜLLER
– Packster 40

Since 1993, the German manufacturer Riese & Müller has produced e-bikes, e-cargo bikes, and folding bikes. Their new Packster 40 is a crossover model with an 18.89-inch-wide (48 cm) cargo area and a total weight of less than 66 lbs (30 kg). Thanks to multiple configuration options, the Packster 40 comes ready for all types of use and is light enough to carry up stairs or to lift onto a car rack when the front wheel has been removed. Its clever dual battery technology means that there are always two batteries on board, giving the bike an unbelievable range of 1000 Wh. LED lighting, disc brakes, and a Bosch Performance Line CX motor are standard issue with the Packster 40. <

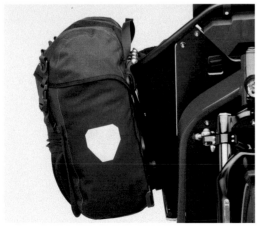

BIOMEGA
– PEK

Copenhagen-based Biomega builds premium bicycles designed to compete with cars and to change the way society defines transportation. Their PEK is a one-size-fits-all cargo commuter, which mixes the features of a city bike with the best assets of a cargo bike. It comes standard with an innovative, super-sized front carrier, which can easily transport daily goods up to 110 lbs (50 kg), a Gates Carbon Drive system, and tires that are 26 inch (66 cm) in the back and 20 inch (51 cm) in the front. Developed specifically for city dwellers, the PEK has a light 39 lbs (18 kg) aluminum frame, and a geometry that holds the body in a slightly inclined position, which delivers navigational ease and exceptional balance. <

– Left: The Biomega BOS 8 speed with a large basket was the inspiration for the **PEK**.
– Above: The fork is painted in glowing florescent paint for extra nighttime visibility.

RETROVELO
— Ponyjohn

The Ponyjohn, designed by **Frank Patitz** for Leipzig-based Retrovelo, is an e-cargo bike developed with maneuverability in mind. Able to carry a maximum load of over 264 lbs (120 kg), the Ponyjohn is incredibly sturdy because of its frame, Taflexa cable steering, and small but wide tires. Inspired by BMX bikes, it has a nearly indestructible two-gear system and is the prototype for Retrovelo's upcoming range of cargo bikes. <

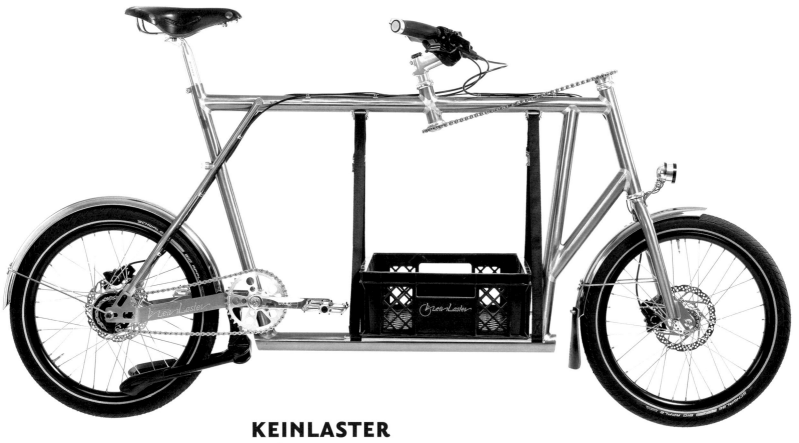

KEINLASTER
– KleinLaster

– Above: Compact design and chain steering.
– Below: The basket is easy to remove and the
bike small enough to take on public transportation.

After realizing that a conventional cargo bike was often too large for her needs, **Nele Dittmar** designed a cargo bike that could effortlessly double as a city bike. The KleinLaster is easy to maneuver, and it can be adjusted in size, depending on its rider's needs. The positioning of the cargo area, as well as the small wheelbase and chain steering, help give the bike a small turning radius, which is advantageous when maneuvering heavy loads. Weighing only 37 lbs (17 kg), the 75-inch (190 cm) bike is light enough to take up and down stairs and can even fit on a train. <

CRANKING UP California's BICYCLE Revolution

— Frances Cycles

Inspired by California's sun and surf, Frances Cycles' **Joshua Muir** *is an advocate of cycling as an alternative mode of transport. His touring and cargo bikes make the concept an attractive one.*

A visit to the workshop of Joshua Muir, in the coastal city of Santa Cruz, is like taking a step back to a simpler era: chickens and ducks greet you, scratching through a yard shaded by persimmon and avocado trees, while Muir's cat eyes you from a private vantage point. There is an abundance of sun-bleached wooden

and tin textures, old tools, and a distinct impression of engineering and endeavor. Muir, a California native, obviously feels very much at home in this environment.

California has long been a hotbed of alternative thought and lifestyle. Although the state is still very much governed by the automotive industry, with

most of the populace traveling by car for even short distances—as do most Americans—there's an active community of optimistic commuters enjoying the benefits of traveling by bicycle. It's growing too, and this is where Frances Cycles has found its niche: well-crafted cargo and touring bikes that are resilient

– *This page:* Joshua Muir with his **Grinduro bike** (named after an amateur race) and his **Farfarer** trailer.
– *Left:* The **Smallhaul** is an award-winning cargo bike. This version features a performance-oriented setup.

Each new model from FRANCES CYCLES starts out as a simple sketch on a sheet of paper before coming to life IN STEEL.

– *Top left:* Standing in front of the Frances Cycle workshop, which is filled with old machining treasures.
– *Left:* The **Platypus**, a mid-gravity cargo bike.
– *Top:* The fully equipped randonneur **Tourist** with Farfarer trailer has customized tube set and geometry for better fit in its intended use.

and reliable. Having a father in the Air Force meant that Muir moved around a lot as a child, before settling in Santa Cruz. He worked as both a carpenter and a messenger for about 10 years, until a job in a bike shop introduced him to the world of steel fabrication. That,

combined with a love of making things with his hands, led him to his current vocation. While he never had any formal training, he received invaluable instruction from Paul Sadoff of Rock Lobster Cycles, another Santa Cruz local.

Sadoff instructed Muir in the traditional methods of fillet and lug brazing techniques, which Muir still utilizes today. Each new Frances Cycles model starts out as a simple sketch on a sheet of paper, before being translated into steel. Every customer is measured to ensure the

FRANCES CYCLES

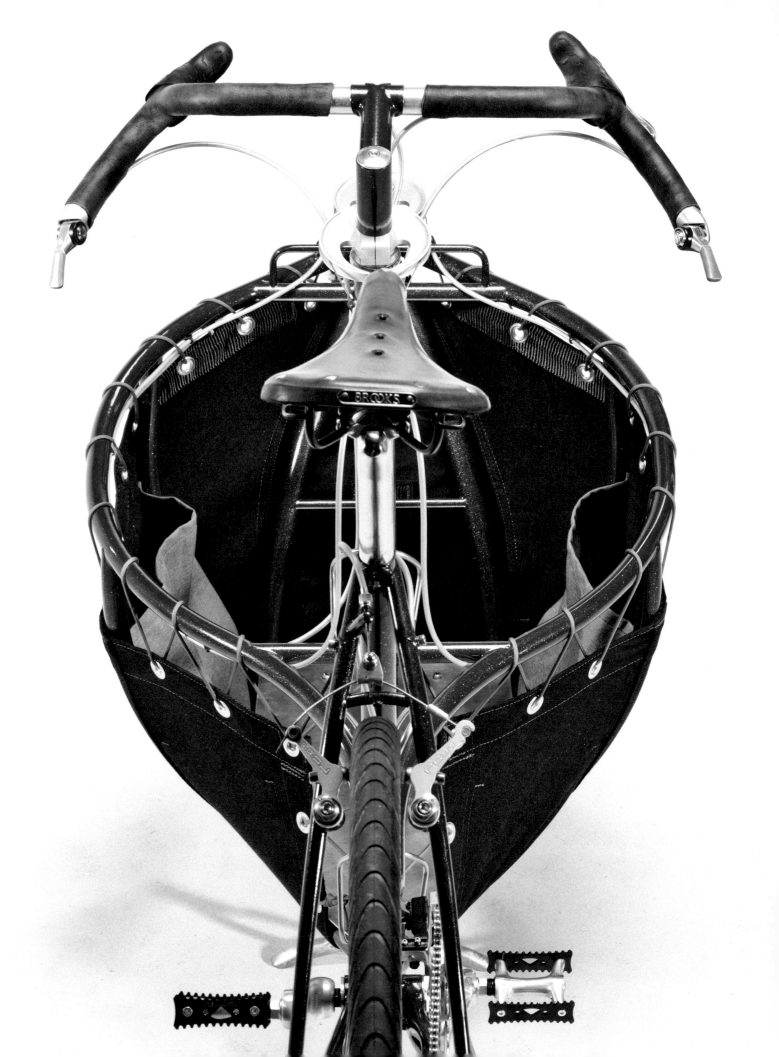

– *Left:* **Smallhaul** is the sportster of cargo hauling, its low cargo hold, which is front and center makes it easy to reach and ideal for touring with a dog or weekend groceries.

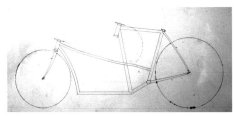

frame is a perfect fit. Numerous options are available, for features such as water bottle cages, disc or caliper brakes, forks, fenders, preferred tire clearances, kickstands, and rack arrangements. Frances Cycles' bikes are recognized by various innovations: the awarded Mixtehaul (Long Diamond Frame) and Smallhaul (Long John) bikes are steered by a cable and pulley system, no longer needing a continuous steering column from the handlebars to the forks. This allows the front wheel to be set forward from the rest of the frame, leaving

FRANCES CYCLES

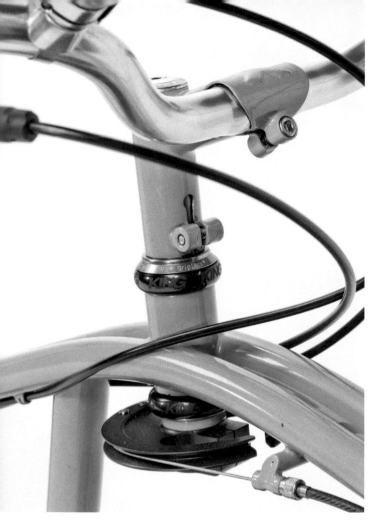

– *Bottom:* The **Mixtehaul** setup comes with a waxed canvas bag and rainfly that snaps to the platform. Other features include cable steering, lighting, fenders, rear rack mounts, and a center stand.

Frances Cycles has found its NICHE: well-crafted cargo and touring bikes that are resilient and RELIABLE.

room for a spacious cargo bay. The Platypus model (a mid-gravity cargo) has similar dimensions to a regular bike, resulting in one of the most agile cargo bikes available. The Tourist model is an elegant touring frameset featuring Muir's trademark outward curved seat stays, which offer an amount of compliance greatly appreciated after many miles in the saddle. The Farfarer one-wheeled trailer can carry a 9-foot surfboard and has a quick release system, while Muir's hand-carved head badges are a personal touch you'd never find on a Prius. Perhaps, if more Californians invested in a Frances cycle instead of another car, a real revolution could begin. <

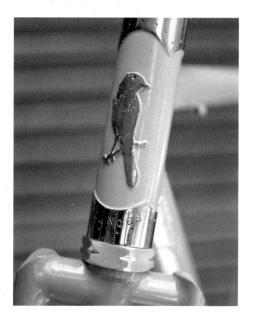

**Muir's hand-carved
head badges are a
PERSONAL TOUCH
you'd never find
on a Prius.**

SVEN CYCLES
– The Forager

When foraging enthusiasts **Darron Coppin, Hugh Fearnley-Whittingstall,** and **Gill Meller** came together to design a bicycle that had everything a forager could want for collecting wild food, they really thought of everything. The low-maintenance Forager, built by Sven Cycles, tackles all manner of terrain with its innovative front wheel that ensures a smooth and safe ride on rough ground. A power hub provides the Forager with a USB charger and lights; and, of course, the Forager is outfitted with the specialty equipment needed by any respectable forager. This includes a BBQ, recyclable plates and utensils, stainless steel water bottles, cutting board, mushroom knife, sharpening stone, foraging hook, hip flask, and bespoke bags by Restrap. <

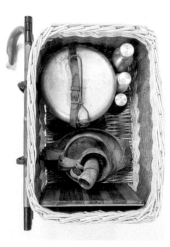

– *Left:* The USB charger sources power from the hub-dynamo.
– *Top:* Custom made bags carry everything needed for a spontaneous picnic or BBQ.

SURLY BIKES
— Big Dummy

For anyone looking for a bicycle that can replace an SUV, Big Dummy by Surly Bikes is it. This long-tail cargo bike can haul a serious amount of stuff. Its single-piece frame, made from 4130 Chromoly steel, can carry about 200 lbs (90 kg) of cargo, and is stiff and resistant to torsional flex, which provides a comfortable ride. The high-quality parts kit includes a 3 × 10 drivetrain, Avid BB7 disc brakes, Shimano DEORE hubs, and 26 × 2.3 inch Kenda Kiniption tires. Surly-designed bags, deck, and Dummy Rail Collars carry everything from groceries to guitars. <

The Future of Cycling is ELECTRIC

The e-bike isn't here to clash with cycle culture. Its strength does not lie in hand-welded steel frames and retro accessories, but unfolds under the lens of city life. Urban challenges like congestion and air pollution make the electric bicycle shine bright. A cheaper and less stressful alternative to driving a car, and considered by some even more fun than riding a bike, it has still taken two decades for e-bikes to sell. Only now, after a rebrand, is the e-bike's reputation beginning to improve.

COBOC—ONE BROOKLYN ⟶ p. 156

E-bikes used to be mostly step-through frames with electric components attached to them. It wasn't a great look. Today's electric bicycles, with their refined technology, have a far broader appeal. They've become design objects in their own right. There are electric urban bikes, cargo bikes, folding bikes, beach cruisers, hi-tech mountain bikes, and even road bikes with tiny motors hidden—inside the frame. They deliver a powerful feel, as their use extends beyond the range of the regular bicycle. The new cycling speaks to commuters and to tech-savvy and climate-conscious urbanites alike. Countries where bike culture is prevalent, such as Germany, Denmark, Belgium, the Netherlands, and France, have embraced e-bikes. In Holland alone, almost 30% of all new bicycles sold are electric. Even the U. K. is getting in on the game, with e-bike sales increasing 220% in 2017. Worldwide, to date, over 35 million electric bicycles and scooters have made it onto the road; and by 2025, that number is expected to rise by another 50%. E-bikes tap into a basic need for mobility and convenience, and, on top of that, they're ideal for personal transport when living the city life.

The Japanese first pushed the convenience of cycling when Yamaha jumped on the e-bike saddle in the early nineties. Yamaha's engineers had their minds trained on mothers who cycle their kids to school (a collective exercise observed across Japan to this day) on a bike called a mamachari. An electric version was developed, with a focus on making mom's life easier. The low-tech solution of a simple motion sensor, which rewards a few lazy revolutions of the pedal with an extra push, did the trick. Today, however, most e-bikes have a torque sensor that precisely measures the force a cyclist puts on the pedal. The English call this principle "pedal-assist." The feeling resembles walking or running up an escalator, and the motor matches only the power that is put into it, thus making the rider feel a little like a superhero. With an e-bike, a hill seems to flatten, and acceleration is a rush.

The early easy ride image e-bikes inherited from the mamachari would, however, prove a persistent problem. When electric cycles first landed in Europe, the cycling community had just found a new love for mountain bikes, and e-bikes got branded "granny bikes." Admittedly, they looked the part. Still, in mountainous Switzerland, they caught on early, with local brands like Flyer, and later, called Biketec. A tiny scene concerned with sustainable transport emerged. Inventors came up with their own fast machines, like the Dolphin, and with few regulatory ties at the time, innovation started to take off.

The growing number of electric bicycles eventually came into the focus of regulators, and today most e-bikes fall under the classification of a pedelec 25 (for pedal-electric cycle). Under certain conditions, this category counts them as regular bicycles. The electric motor, for example, must seize to assist at 16 mph (25 km/h), with a 10% leeway. Once the display hits 17 mph (27.5 km/h), the rider falls back on his or her own power. There are e-bikes, however, which deliver up to 28 mph (45 km/h) on pedal-assist, manufactured by companies such as Stromer, who brands them as speed pedelecs. They sit in the same legal niche as mopeds, requiring a license plate, bright lights, and use of a helmet. Cycle lanes are taboo for pedelecs 45 in most countries. Despite the restrictions, the category regularly inspires concept e-bike manufacturers, such as Stealth and Trefecta, to push into motorcycle territory with their machines.

Apart from regulations, and torque sensors lending a more natural cycling feel, there is another component to the pedelec's success—better batteries. Once again, engineers from Japan were called upon to find an alternative to the bulky, heavy, lead-acid batteries with which early e-bikes were equipped. NiMH and today's Lithium-ion cells, like the ones in laptops and electric cars, were introduced. Small in size but capable of holding a lot of energy, an e-bike battery can now last for 50–62 miles (80–100 km), and it's compact enough to fit snugly onto a frame or even be hidden inside it.

Motor development took off as well, after Austrian company KTM put powerful BionX rear-wheel

STROMER—ST2

drive on mountain bikes. Large automotive suppliers like Bosch and Brose came into the market around 2012, and their strong central drives took e-bikes to a new level. Bosch now has four lines of motors at different performance levels. Brose targets smaller series and allowed Specialized to boost its hi-tech electric MTB with its own take on the software, which guarantees that the e-bike can master any rock and curve on a trail almost naturally. Electronics have become the bicycle's second nature.

This new tech and feel allows designers to play. VanMoof, Faraday, and Coboc fully integrate electric

TREFECTA MOBILITY—DRT SPEED PEDELEC ⟶ p. 160

Bosch, Pendix and Brose are all examples of companies that originally produced car parts and are now expanding into the growing electric bike movement.

EXPERT ESSAY—*Electric Bikes*

components and Fazua even makes its own compact crank drive. Sleek bikes such as these attract a new breed of consumer, one who loves the ease of an electric bike, but doesn't want to flash their motor or battery. After all, who likes to be obvious? Not to mention, the image of "cheating" has never really left the e-bike, and most style-conscious consumers like the extra power to be invisible.

Seen from the perspective of a road cyclist or courier on a fixie, a pedelec may look like cheating indeed. In fact, the UCI banned a cyclocross rider in 2016, when referees discovered a motor hidden inside her bike. The Tour de France now regularly uses X-rays to check for mechanical doping. Still, electric mountain and road bikes sales are up, especially among those turning 40 and above who want to continue to cycle the Alps.

But leisure aside, simply getting from A to B quickly, easily, and sustainably is an issue many commuters face; and cities, most of all, would like to see people getting on bikes. This is not an easy task, but e-bikes may be the compromise a non-cyclist needs. With a pedelec, the nine mile (15 km) jaunt to the workplace does not seem too far; and arriving at the office drenched in sweat becomes a choice, not a given. Naturally, those who already cycle a lot won't feel the difference as much as the untrained hobby cyclist; and the assisted top speed of 16 mph (25 km/h) won't impress people that ride that fast. In the U.S., some states have raised the speed limit to 20 mph. That's about 30 km/h, a pretty perfect speed to swim with city traffic. S-pedelecs, such as the ones from Klever, target commuters directly, and offer range and speeds hard to beat on a bicycle. However, a regular e-bike is enough to make cycling in the city easier. During London's rush hour, for example, cars go no faster than 16 mph (25 km/h) on average anyway; and in that slow flow,

Simply getting from A to B quickly, easily, and sustainably is an issue many commuters face.

VANMOOF ⟶ p. 140

DIAMANT—ZOUMA ELITE+ S ⟶ p. 150

ETT INDUSTRIES—TRAYSER ⟶ p. 146

With so many urbanites, private cars transporting just one person at a time won't be a viable option for much longer.

electric bicycles still jump the queue the second the light turns green.

Faster cycling poses its own problems. Most Swedes, for example, ride no faster than 7 mph (12 km/h), half the speed a pedelec hits rather easily. To avoid crashes, planners have begun to accommodate the new vehicles taking to the roads at high speeds. The Netherlands is building extra cycle paths. In Taiwan, dedicated scooter lanes may easily be shared with fast electric bicycles. Infrastructure is not the only issue; people have to get used to the new tune of cycling. Towns in France, Sweden, and Italy now include electric two-wheelers in their e-mobility subsidies, while Copenhagen, Madrid, and San Francisco have set up e-bike sharing schemes. Such systems help riders get around the high price of these cycles. A decent pedelec starts at $1,400 (€1,100)

and can easily climb to $3,500 (€2,850) or more.

Spreading the use of e-bikes ever wider is also a nod to the future. Cities with illegally high levels of air pollution, and constant pressure to reduce traffic, see e-bikes as a means to bring down emissions and free up space on the road. As of now, 50% of the earth's population crowds together in cities; and the UN projects that by 2050 that figure will increase to 75%. With so many urbanites, private cars transporting just one person at a time won't

be a viable option for much longer. The future belongs to shared cars and the even more economic, and more likely, electric two-wheelers. To live in a city will mean logging on to its transport network. Connected vehicles will recognize one another, while their passengers and riders will be able to get in on the conversation via mobile devices. For e-bikes, apps already turn a smartphone into a hi-tech display; and parts such as the Copenhagen Wheel sense pollution and help to navigate around it. E-bikes are digitized already, and

with tech being at the core, many a cycle purist has tried to discount them entirely, likening them to computers that killed the typewriter. For now, though, it seems as if bicycles and electric bikes can co-exist with ease, just as vinyl does with digital audio files. There will be more diffusion of technology into the bicycle as that technology becomes ever more sensible and the connection between humans and machines grows ever tighter. And who is to say that a bike with a motor to match muscles (and maybe brainwaves) isn't cycling too?

— by Nora Manthey

VANMOOF
– Electrified S, X-Frame

Founded by brothers **Taco** and **Ties Carlier**, Netherlands-based VanMoof specializes in building city bikes with custom parts designed in the company workshop. Their revolutionary Electrified S sports a light frame filled with integrated technology, such as lights and anti-theft features, including an integrated e-lock, G-sensor detect tampering detection, anti-theft nuts and bolts, and built-in location tracking. The bike features a boost-button on the handlebar, which pulls the front wheel drive bike up to 20 mph (32 km/h). A hidden stainless steel chain, unbreakable tires, disc-brakes, and an app all come in the standard package. <

– *Left:* The **VanMoof Electrified S** with an optional Bambooman front rack, which can carry loads up to 22 lbs (10 kg). The bike also has a 250 W motor in the front hub and a battery capacity of 418 Wh.

PURE CYCLES
– Volta

The Volta e-bike by Pure Cycles is the company's next step toward convincing more people to ride e-bikes. Its 40-mile (64 km) range and unique design make riding simple. Top features include remote activation, activity tracking, regenerative braking, environmentally adaptive performance modes, and GPS security tracking. The Volta's rear-mounted motor keeps the bike balanced, while an automatic headlight ensures safety in low light conditions. The integrated front basket accommodates heavy loads without sacrificing stability. <

TSINOVA
– ION

Tsinova's ION is a rule-breaking e-bike whose unique trapezoid body design marks a departure from the traditional triangular frame. As a result, vibrations are transmitted to the rear of the bike, which provides enhanced riding comfort. The ION's adoption of belt-driven systems also offers a smooth and quiet riding experience. Haptic highlighting and Brooks parts combine with a variety of high-tech components, including a VeloUP power system, updates via cloud, GPS tracker, and onboard diagnosis (OBD). The Panasonic battery can be charged in just about two hours and delivers power up to 43 miles (70 km) at 15 mph (25 km/h) maximum speed. Weighing in at just 31 lbs (14 kg), the ION is almost half the weight of a traditional e-bike. <

ETT INDUSTRIES
— Trayser

Originally founded in New Zealand, ETT Industries eventually established itself as a UK-based company dedicated to making electric transportation solutions for the modern urban lifestyle. Its first product, the Trayser, is an e-bike offering a wide range of personalization through its 3D-printed accessories. Along with its unique appearance, the patented aluminum monocoque frame provides supreme functionality, including a 90-mile (145 km) range. With a charging time of three and a half hours, and top speeds of 15.5 mph (25 km/h), the Trayser is an innovative e-bike designed to take riders into the future of transportation. <

DIAMANT
– Zouma Elite+ S

Diamant's Zouma Elite+ S is its first pedelec with the capability of reaching speeds of up to 28 mph (45 km/h). Weighing in at just over 57 lbs (26 kg), the sport pedelec has a Bosch Performance Line Speed integrated 500 W battery, an Ecomodus range of 39 miles (63 km), Magura MT5 hydraulic disc brakes, and a NuVinci N380 step-less hub. Also included in the standard build are Supernova lights, a Brooks saddle, ergonomic grips, side stand, racks, mud guards, integrated wiring, and bulky Schwalbe Super Moto-X tires that work great on any terrain. <

DESIKNIO
– Urban Classic

Desiknio creates stylish, high-quality electric bikes from its workshop in Granada, Spain. With an emphasis on precision, stability, and safety, designer **Joaquin Cortes** produces bikes that offer a sporty ride, with a hidden electric drivetrain. Their Urban Classic frame, weighing just 30 lbs (13.5 kg), is handcrafted from aluminum. A battery in the lower tube delivers power to the rear hub motor at a maximum range of 50 miles (80 km). Everything on the Urban Classic can be monitored by an app. <

LAVELLE BIKES
— The Power Bike

The Power Bike from Lavelle is an e-bike designed to liberate the urban commuter with a nimble, speedy, and safe design. Beating traffic is easy with its strong, lightweight carbon frame, featuring a one-sided fork, a seamlessly integrated 500 W battery lasting up to 60 miles (100 km), automatic transmission, a high torque 250 W Brose system for either 16 mph (25 km/h) or 28 mph (45 km/h), and Magura 2-piston hydraulic disc brakes. The upright frame geometry is unisex; and the squashy gel saddle and balloon tires cushion the bumps on worn out city streets. Additional features include an anti-theft and cloud-connected GPS with turn-by-turn route planning. <

FLASH
– Flash Bike

When the San Francisco-based founders of Flash started designing their e-bike from the ground up, they took a hard look at the issues that stop people from riding bicycles. The Flash Bike solves those issues with a combination of power, safety, security, and intelligence. A 500 W motor and lithium ion battery ensure speed and range, while 360° running lights, automatic brake lights, LED headlight, and turn signals light the way. With its movement-sensitive alarm and GPS tracking device, would-be thieves keep their distance. Wireless connectivity and a touchscreen with pin code make it the most intelligent bicycle on the road and a pleasure to ride. <

– *Above:* The touchscreen in the frame works as a navigation system, e-lock with pin code, and battery level indicator.
– *Right:* Owners can track down a lost or stolen bike via GPS and the bike's own app.

COBOC
– ONE Brooklyn & SEVEN Montreal

Coboc is an award-winning young company from Heidelberg, Germany, with a focus on building minimal, high-quality e-bikes. All of their bikes have the Coboc E-Drive in common, which measures the effort the rider puts on the crank via a Torque sensor. From the bike's app, the rider can choose between different modes, including start-boost, constant power, or gain. The battery is made from LG cells (352 kWh), which are also used by Tesla, and which have an average range of 50 miles (80 km). The hub motor is one of the lightest at 6 lbs (2.7 kg). The ONE Brooklyn features a single speed, a maintenance-free belt, and a carbon fiber fork. The SEVEN Montreal has an integrated rack, TRP slate disc brakes, Curana C-Lite fenders, seven gears, and an integrated LED tail light. <

ENKI CYCLES
– Billy e-Bike

At San Francisco-based Enki Cycles, the focus is always on a fun ride. Billy is a BMX at its core but garnished with all the ingredients to create a super leisure companion. Made from aluminium, the bike is light, weighing in at 48.5 lbs (22 kg). Four colour options are available in polished aluminum, stealth black, billy blue and arctic white. For a ninja-like ride it has a Gates carbon belt drive, adjustable suspension, a 500 W fat bike motor which is powered by a 13,6Ah Samsung Li-Ion battery. This set up is good for a 41 mile (66 km) range at 20 mph (32 km/h). 20 inch weight reduced wheels paired with super light tyres reduce rotational mass and improve acceleration. Five customizable levels of power control dictate how much power is transferred by the hyper responsive twist throttle. Finally, the best feature just might be the fully foldable frame. <

COWBOY
– Cowboy Bike

After their food delivery company went belly up, **Adrien Roose** and **Karim Slaoui** joined forces with **Tanguy Goretti** to found Cowboy, an electric bike company looking to increase the popularity of e-bikes through superior pricing, quality product design, and technology. Automatic motor assistance and a smart battery are standard features on the Cowboy Bike. It also has its own app, which controls power to the bike, serves as a GPS tracking system, and provides theft detection. By developing its own technology, Cowboy has greater control over its product design and production costs; and while its direct sales model ensures lower prices and a better connection with customers. <

TREFECTA MOBILITY
– DRT Speed Pedelec & DRT Off-Road Unlimited

Netherlands-based Trefecta develops and produces reliable and robust e-bikes with modular designs that can traverse the toughest terrains while still standing the test of time. Their DRT Off-road Unlimited and DRT Speed Pedelec, designed by **Norbert Haller**, showcase these qualities to the max. E-bikes absent of compromise, and filled with innovative features, boasting a hybrid drivetrain, regenerative brakes, a frame made from aerospace-grade aluminum, carbon fiber wheels, and a handlebar display. All of this comes with a peak motor power of 4 kW, top speeds of 44 mph (70 km/h), and a range of 35 miles (55 km). <

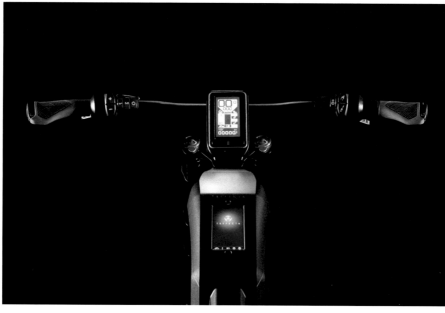

– Right: The **DRT Off Road Unlimited** overlooking Monaco. With speeds of up to 44 mph (70 km/h), a helmet and gloves are highly recommended.
– Left top: The **DRT Speed Pedelec** reaches speeds of 28 mph (45 km/h) and has a 62 miles (100 km) range.

NOORDUNG
– Noordung One

Noordung takes its name from the pioneering Slovenian rocket engineer Herman Potocnik (1892–1929), an inspiration for both the bike company and Stanley Kubrick. Potocnik's nickname, meaning "no order" in a combination of English and German, reflects the company's free spirit and appreciation of heritage. With its carbon fiber frame, the Noordung One is amongst the lightest e-bikes on the market, at 34 lbs (15.4 kg). It reinvents the cycling experience with a removable boom box and a battery which provides power to pedal assistance via the Vivax Assist 4.75 at 200 watts. USB ports for charging come standard, but the weirdest feature is the dust sensor that constantly checks for air pollution. Two versions are available. The Moonlight Edition with a black frame and silver boom-box or inverted color combination known as the Eclipse Edition. <

NICOLAI BICYCLES
– ION-G16 EBOXX

After many years in development, the Nicolai ION-G16 EBOXX made its debut in 2017. It is the first bike ever to have the unique combination of the newest Bosch CX Performance motor and a race-tested and pace-casted Geometron chassis with a battery hidden in the frame. Bulletproof SRAM components are the first choice for smooth shifting. Developed in close cooperation with FOX, the geometry delivers plenty of traction in corners and extraordinary grip on steep climbs. Compared to traditional MTB geometry, the bike has a lower center of gravity and a longer wheelbase, resulting in a smoother ride. <

Nicolai began building racing bikes in 1995 for the MTB World Cup. Since 2009, the company has been a leader in e-bike development.
– *Opposite left*: Beautifully executed welding and integrated cables.
– *Right*: CNC's suspension detail was specially developed for the bike, which weighs 55 lbs (25 kg) when dry.

NEEMATIC
– FR/1

Neematic's FR/1 is a high-performance, all-terrain e-bike whose electronic drive technology gives it the power of a small motorcycle but the versatility of a mountain bike. Designer **Linas Kraniauskas** and team developed this new experience by creating a unique e-bike that delivers 15 kW from its mid-drive motor. Operated by twist throttle and pedal assist modes (9-speed Pinion gearbox for pedaling), massive jumps are an easy task for the FOX shocks. The 115 lbs (52 kg) bike can reach 50 mph (80 km/h) at top speed; and the 2.2 kWh li-ion battery pack takes 2.5 hours to charge. Adjustable regenerative braking and LCD display come as no surprise in this fun-packed gem. <

LITHIUM CYCLES
– The Super 73® Scout

Based in Southern California, Lithium Cycles is a lifestyle company that designs, manufactures, and distributes electric transportation for rugged trails, sandy beaches, urban commuting, and other short distance adventures. Launched in 2016, the company was one of many e-bike start-ups looking to change cycling with a new kind of electric hybrid bike. Using cutting-edge technology, and inspired by the rich heritage of minibike culture from the 1970s, Lithium's Super 73® electric bikes are as simple as can be. The fun starts at $1,400 (€1,140) and the bikes don't even require a license or registration. <

LEADING the CHARGE

— Vintage Electric Bikes

Are these retro-styled, futuristic machines motorcycles or bicycles? The e-bike blurs the line between the two; and California's Vintage Electric Bikes will leave you wanting to flick the power switch.

E-bikes have arrived, and they're here to stay, but at this embryonic stage of their evolution, their aesthetic has struggled to find a voice. They still remain the oddball offspring of European and Asian engineers, more focused on technology than on creating a vehicle that gets the heart racing. Back in 2011, however, Vintage Electric Bike's founder, Andrew Davidge, had the vision to combine the timeless culture of the American cruiser with an electric motor; and his synthesis was a success.

Davidge assembled his first e-bike in his parents' garage while he was still in school, which ultimately gave him the impetus to start Vintage Electric Bikes. After seven years of business, the bikes are sold through a global dealer network and have a massive fan base. Customers include Hollywood A-list celebrities, tree-huggers, and every demographic in between. Every model is designed in Santa Clara, California; and the heart of the bikes—the battery cases—are sand-cast up the road in San Jose.

CUSTOMERS include Hollywood **A-LIST** celebrities, tree-huggers, and every demographic in **BETWEEN**.

– *Above:* The **Emory Outlaw Tracker** is a limited edition produced in partnership with Emory Motorsports, the go-to workshop for Porsche 356.
– *Left:* The **Tracker** in Indy Red.
– *Right:* Each bike is hand assembled in California and features easy throttle control with your thumb.

Housed inside the case is a 702 W hour L-ion battery, which takes approximately two hours to charge. The battery is good for a 35-mile (56 km) range and a top speed of 20 mph (32 km/h)—plenty of grunt for keeping up with traffic around town. For those seeking an extra boost, a Race Mode option deploys a 3,000 W rear hub motor at the flick of a switch, silently accelerating the rider to a grin-inducing 35 mph (56 km/h). Just be sure to check the speed limit on public roads— e-bike legislation is still nebulous, to say the least. The rest of the bike is composed of top-shelf components: MRP suspension forks, Phil Wood front hubs, and leather accoutrements from Brooks England. Vintage Electric e-bikes are the most iconic in design on the road today, equipped with the best components

For those seeking an EXTRA BOOST, the Race Mode option deploys a 3,000 W rear hub motor at the flick of a switch.

– *Opposite left:* The beach-inspired **Cruz** with maple wood inlay.
– *Left and top:* The **Cafe** comes with integrated Supernova LED lighting and silently propels its rider with five different assist levels. The aluminum battery box is removeable for easy charging.

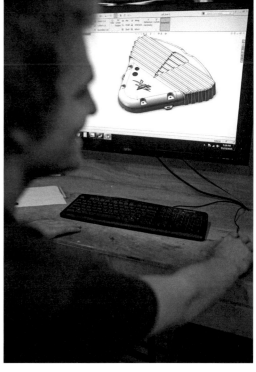

available. But there's also a range of upgrades and accessories on offer: rear luggage racks and waterproof panniers, a toolbox or leather Brooks saddle bag, LED tail lights, helmets, and suspension forks.

The Cruz model, which features an authentic maple side panel inlay and integrated lighting, is priced at approximately $7,000 (€5,600) with all its bells and whistles. Considering the quality of the construction, and the list of parts, the price point is fair. Though you could buy a small car for the same price, you're buying a whole truckload of integrity in a Vintage Electric Bike, not to mention guilt-free transport. <

RUFF CYCLES
– The Ruffian e-Bike

When custom cycle brand Ruff Cycles got Bosch e-drives, they went straight to work designing an all-new bike; and within six months, the Ruffian e-bike was ready to go. After a speedy round of testing and certification, the new creation was launched, to the excitement of the brand's devoted fans. Beach cruisers are known for their energy-consuming weight, but modern technology ensures that Ruffian's vintage-looking cruiser rides light and fast. <

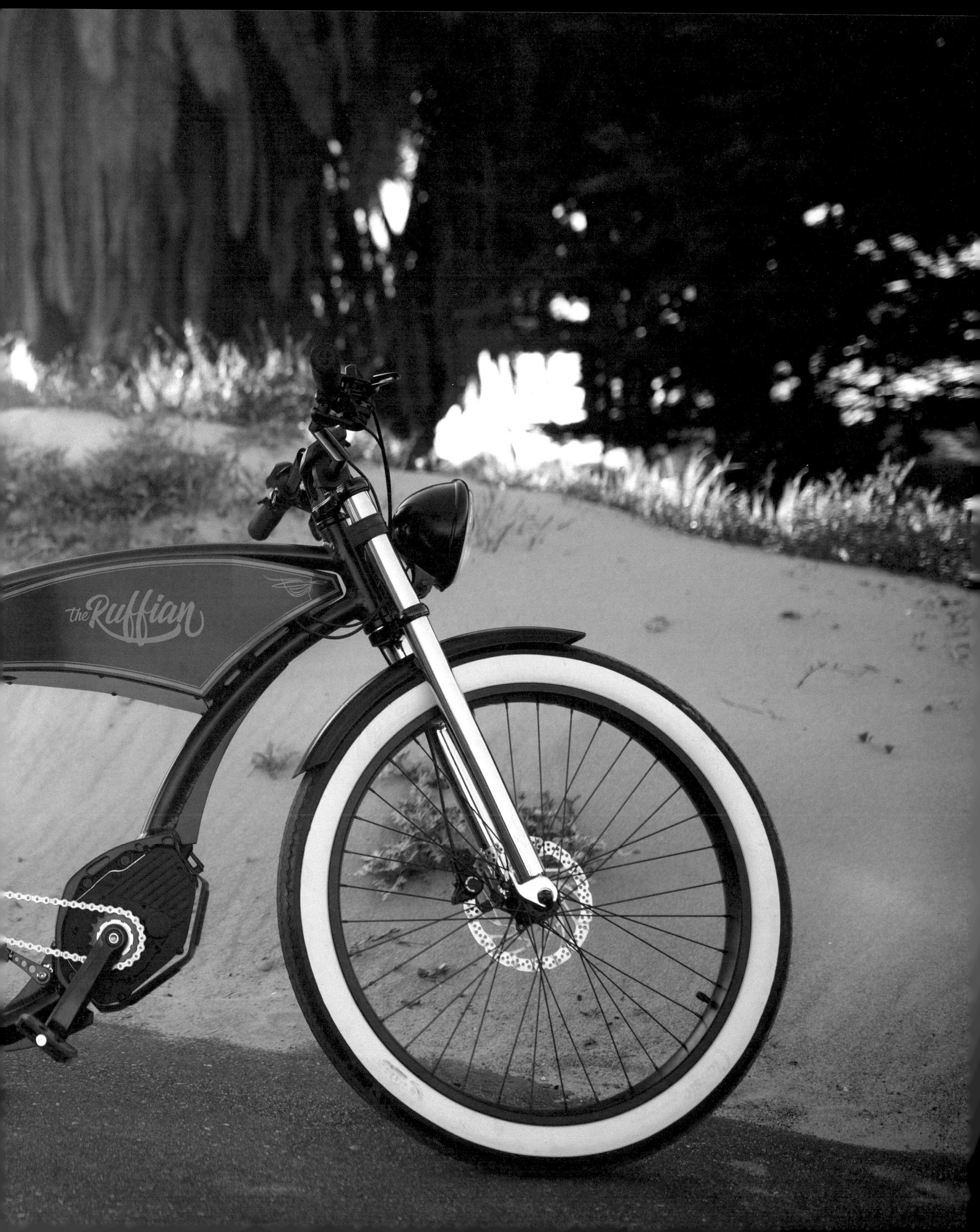
the Ruffian

MATTEO DE MAYDA
– Bici Palermo Tuning

Intrigued by the teenaged founders of Bici Palermo Tuning, the photographer **Matteo de Mayda** set out to document the bicycles they modify with speakers and amplifiers. Using car batteries for power, the boys ride around the city of Palermo blasting Neapolitan music. The ultimate goal of the young members of this club is to see who can build the loudest sound system, with some spending up to $1,600 (€1,300) on their hi-fi bicycle modifications. <

MATTEO DE MAYDA—*Bici Palermo Tuning*

Bicycle Basics, Selection, and MAINTENANCE

So you've decided to commute by bicycle. Good for you! Cycling combines exercise, transportation, mental health benefits, environmental sustainability, and thrifty economics. It's a wonder why more people don't ride, but that's another story.

Here are some things you'll need to keep in mind before and after getting a bike:

1) Types of bikes: frame geometry and materials
2) Fitting your bike to your body
3) Basic maintenance and upkeep
4) Security
5) City riding basics

1) TYPES OF BIKES

Frame Geometry

Contrary to popular opinion, one bicycle does not fit all. Not only do bikes come in different sizes, but different shapes as well; these shapes will dictate what type of riding you'll be doing.

Frame geometry affects the position of the rider on the bike, and different riding positions are beneficial for different types of riding. Road bike geometry, where the head tube and seat tube angles are quite steep, pitches the rider forward, which allows for maximum efficiency in pedaling output. Touring geometry is more relaxed to allow for long rides in the saddle, while a town bike's geometry puts the rider in an almost upright riding position, which is great for viewing traffic. There is an entire spectrum of riding positions, and myriad subdivisions in the types of frames out there—people will argue for days about them. Many people ride road bikes to work; and it's not unheard of for people to take Dutch-style bikes touring. Just know that if you're just starting out as a commuter, getting a commuter-specific bike, like a hybrid or a step-through, will be your best bet. From there you'll be able to tell if you want something racier—or not. If you're on the fence, ask to try out friends' bikes, and always test ride a bike before buying.

Frame Materials

The first bikes were made from steel, but with advancements in metal alloys and carbon, bikes are now made from aluminum, carbon fiber, and even bamboo. Different materials provide different "ride-feel." Aluminum (a.k.a. alloy) bikes are the most common, as the material is lightweight and cheap. But guess what it's not: comfortable. Aluminum transfers vibrations easily, and bumps from the road travel straight up to the rider. As they say in the industry: strong, light, and cheap—choose two. Carbon is strong and light, but not cheap. It's good at dampening vibrations, but not as good as lightweight steel. Steel is light and strong, but the good stuff ain't cheap, and the cheap stuff is heavy. If you're just starting out, there's nothing wrong with an aluminum frame. You can always upgrade in the future.

2) FITTING YOUR BIKE TO YOUR BODY

While you can spend hundreds on a professional bike fitting, there are simple ways to gauge if a bike frame is the right size for you. Start off by measuring your height and your inseam. Here's a basic chart used for road bikes (please note that there are extra size charts for mountain-bikes, BMX, and others, because their general geometry is different according to their type of use: You can quickly see if a bike will fit you when you test out a model. If it has a

DETERMINING YOUR COMMUTER BIKE FRAME SIZE

Rider height	Leg inseam	Suggested frame size
4.1–5.1 in / 147–155 cm	24–29 in / 61–73 cm	14 in / 47–49 cm
5.1–5.5 in / 155–165 cm	25–30 in / 63–76 cm	15 in / 50–52 cm
5.5–5.9 in / 165–175 cm	26–31 in / 66–78 cm	16 in / 53–54 cm
5.9–6.0 in / 175–183 cm	27–32 in / 68–81 cm	17 in / 55–57 cm
6.0–6.3 in / 183–191 cm	28–33 in / 71–83 cm	18 in / 58–61 cm
6.1–6.6 in / 191–198 cm	29–34 in / 73–86 cm	19 in / 61–63 cm

The size chart above works for regular commuter/hybrid bicycles. Please note, that frame characteristics from mountain bikes and road bikes may vary, but you can find them all online. Buying bicycles online is getting popular, saves money and works. The old salesmen saying "try your bike first" is not 100% applicable anymore.

perfectly horizontal top tube, stand astride the bar and make sure you have about an inch between your crotch and the tube. Too wide a gap, and the bike is too small; too small a gap, and the bike is too big. You can probably choose a bike that's a teensy bit too big or small for you, as there are other points on the bike that can be adjusted to make it fit your body.

In fact, there are three contact points to adjust: your butt, your hands, and your feet. If you're riding in a city, you'll want to be able to put your foot on the ground easily as you come to a stop. Adjust your saddle height to make sure you can do this easily. If your saddle is too high, your hips will start to see-saw side to side, which can cause hip problems. Too low, and your knees will be unhappy, and will probably let you know. You can also move your saddle's fore and aft position to make sure your sit bones (the ones

in your butt) are positioned comfortably. Make sure your saddle is wide enough to accommodate your sit bones, and perfectly horizontal. If the nose is too high, your bits will be in pain, and if the nose is too low, you'll be sliding forward, putting too much pressure on your hands and wrists. Larger professional bike shops often have a saddle measuring system, so if you're having issues, get your bum measured!

You can also move your hand position to change how you fit on your bike. The most comfortable handle-bar, and one which can be used in almost any type of cycling, is what's known as the North Road bar, where the bars sweep up and toward the back of the bike. The bars are wide, to allow for more maneuverability; and hands are kept happy by the ergonomically correct positioning. Drop bars are a popular style, and are great for racing and long distance riding, as they allow for

EXPERT ESSAY—*Bicycle Basics, Selection and Maintenance*

3) BASIC MAINTENANCE AND UPKEEP

There's a difference between maintenance and repair; good maintenance will generally prevent a need for costly repairs. Get your bike serviced once a year at your local bike shop. With home maintenance, think "little and often." Four times a year, at the change of seasons, do these small and simple things to take care of your bike:

3.1) Wipe down your rims with a damp cloth. Dirt and grit from the road builds up, causing brake pads and rims to wear faster. If you have disc brakes, wipe down your rotors with rubbing alcohol, being very careful not to touch them with your hands, as oil from your fingers can compromise braking surfaces.

3.2) Clean your chain. Using rubbing alcohol, or a dedicated chain cleaner, and two old toothbrushes tied together with rubber bands, with the brush heads facing each other, scrub your chain down so that most of the oil, dirt, and grime are removed.

3.3) Lube your chain, but only after you've cleaned it. People often mistakenly think that a lot of oil is good for your chain—it's not. Excess oil attracts dirt and grit, creating a sandpaper-like paste that wears down components faster. Use a biodegradable all-season lubricant, such as "Pedro's Chain." Wet lube is great for mountain biking and wet weather, while dry lube is good for dry weather. Put one drop of lube on each bushing, let it sink in for 15 minutes, and then—this is the most important part—wipe off as much as you can with an old t-shirt. You may even need to wipe off the excess the following day as the oil seeps out. You want the lubricant to be between the metal, not on the outside!

3.4) Pump your tires to their correct pressure using a track pump. Do this every month! Keeping your tires pumped will prevent punctures from potholes and protect your rims. And don't hop curbs unless you have a mountain bike or fat tires—you could end up damaging your rims or spokes.

three different hand positions: on the tops, the hoods, and the drops. You can move your hands around to change your body position, which eases pressure on them. Flat bars are common and wide flat bars in particular are making a comeback, as they are comfortable and allow for more control. If you have short flat bars, the ride-feel is quite twitchy. This style is only recommended for messengers who want to squeeze through traffic. Finally, make sure you've got grips or bar tape. These accessories are not just about aesthetic appeal—they're safety mechanisms there to ensure that you are in control of your bike. Naked bars might look nice, but you can lose your grip easily, especially in the rain. Bar end plugs are also a must, especially with drop bars. If the ends of your bars are exposed, and you get in a crash, the bar will go straight through your thigh, or other parts. It's called "coring" for a reason.

3.1

3.2

3.4

4) SECURITY

You've got your rad bike, now you've got to keep it! Unfortunately, theft is a very real problem in urban areas. Be sure to use a good lock; they say spend 10% of what your bike is worth to you. You can also use two or three different types of locks (such as D-locks, cable locks, or chains) so that a thief will need multiple tools to get to your bike. Get a lock that has a minimum rating of "Sold Secure Silver." If you have bike theft insurance, you'll often be required to use a lock rated "Sold Secure Gold." There are also small locks that live on your bike, securing your wheels, saddle/seat post, and handlebars. Look to brands like Hexlox, Pitlock, and Pinhead for these small but handy types of locks. Park in well-lit areas, but don't depend on the kindness of strangers to keep your bike safe. City folk are busy folk, and probably wouldn't question someone using an angle grinder on a lock—I know because it's happened to me!

Punctures are a matter of when, not if, so make sure you've taught yourself how to replace an inner tube.

5) CITY RIDING BASICS

Punctures are a matter of when, not if, so make sure you've taught yourself how to replace an inner tube. Carry a tool kit containing the following: a spare tube, a puncture kit, a small hand pump, tire levers, a multi-tool, and (if your wheels have locknuts) a 0.6 in (15 mm) spanner. You can patch a punctured tube, turning it into a spare inner tube. I also like to carry around nitrile gloves, zip ties, and some candy to prevent grumpiness. What extra items would you carry in your kit?

Chances are you'll have to carry stuff while you're riding about town. An easy way to do this is to wear a rucksack or messenger bag, but these can get sweaty and gross after a while. Pannier racks and baskets are a great way to transport your things, and I hear bum bags are making a comeback.

They say there's no such thing as bad weather, only inappropriate clothing. When riding in inclement weather, make sure your bike has mudguards, and outfit yourself with a good waterproof jacket and waterproof gloves. There are even rainproof onesies, like the Senscommon and Raynsie. If you really hate the rain, you can wear waterproof pants over your regular ones, and shoe covers. I have a pair of Chelsea rain boots that I save for rainy days, as I hate having wet feet. In an emergency, put some plastic bags over your socks and inside your shoes to keep dry.

And last, but certainly not least, get a set of good lights. When riding in a city, you're more likely to need lights to be seen than to see. (If you're riding on a lone country lane or dirt path, you'll need a high-powered torch.) I actually carry two sets of USB lights at all times so that, when one runs out, I have a spare on me. I also like using side visibility wheel lights, like those from VeloHalo or MonkeyLectric. They really get attention—I've even been complimented by cabbies!

Most importantly, make sure you're having fun. Riding a bike is a beautiful thing, for yourself and for the planet. Enjoy!

— *by Jenni Gwiazdowski*

THE FAMILY that Rides TOGETHER, Designs Together

Bryan Hollingsworth *of Royal H Cycles counts craft, heritage, and his family as influences. He steers the bicycle industry toward quality custom frames that can be passed down to the next generation.*

– *Left:* The **Hollingsworth Light Tourer**, a combination of Uncle Pete's lugs and Bryan's frame building.
– *Right:* Bryan Hollingsworth checks a finished steel fixed gear racer.

Cycling runs deep in the Hollingsworth family's blood. Bryan Hollingsworth celebrated his 14th birthday by riding 100 miles (161 km) with his parents; and his sister and mother have ridden across North America. His first 10-speed bicycle was also his mother's first: a Raleigh Super Grand Prix. His grandfather wasn't a cyclist but a proficient woodworker; and while his uncle

and sister inherited this love for woodwork, Bryan was bestowed with an artisan's eye for finishing—an aesthetic he successfully applies to his steel work.

Hollingsworth doesn't exclusively work with steel. After completing a frame-building course at the United Bicycle Institute, he interned at Boston's Seven Cycles, where he still works today, assembling

their carbon frames. Steel happens to be his preferred medium, as it's the most practical for the everyday cyclist. Hollingsworth believes that aluminum and carbon are perfect for racing, but his personal focus, and that of Royal H Cycles, is on bikes that will last long enough to hand down to the next generation. Since it was founded in 2009, Royal H Cycles has produced

STEEL happens to be his preferred medium, as it's the most PRACTICAL for the everyday cyclist.

- Top right: The **Hollingsworth Clubman** was built by Bryan's uncle, Pete, as a slight update to the British bikes of the 1930s.
- Right: Respecting English tradition puzzling an updated version of the thimble fork and the iconic Raleigh front end with help from Geekhouse bikes.
- Left: Andrew's vintage racer is inspired by the tour bikes of the past and features a primitive drive train.
- Top left: Chauney's rando with 9-speed Campagnolo Chorus.

tourers, track bikes, mountain bikes, mixtes, and randonneurs. Hollingsworth won't balk at bizarre requests or geometries, as the bespoke frame is the backbone of the handmade bicycle market. He's built bikes for very tall riders; a near-reproduction of a complicated French constructeur-style bike, in the spirit of Alex Singer and René Herse; a pair of matching tourers for a husband and wife; and modern all-day road riders and cyclocrossers.

It makes for a colorful portfolio, but Hollingsworth refuses to restrict his customers to a seasonal palette; they themselves present random swatches that dictate their frames' paint. An old man's sweater has inspired the hues of a randonneur, while a customer who worked as a draper once brought a fabric off-cut to the paint booth. What unites these differing styles is the graphic identity of Royal H Cycles: the classical

Hollingsworth refuses to restrict his customers to a SEASONAL palette.

– *Top left*: The overall ice blue color scheme can be found even in the sprockets—note the three reserve spokes.

decals and logos that were all designed by Bryan's uncle, Pete Hollingsworth.

Pete has always supported Bryan's work, and they recently teamed up on more than just the graphics. At the 2015 Philly Bike Expo, Pete sat in on Doug Fattic's lug-carving demo and was hooked. He bought three sets and began shaping them immediately, impressing his nephew. As a result, they conceived a new Royal H Cycles range simply called Hollingsworth, featuring over ten styles of unique lug designs and Bryan's construction. The result is a bike with a golden-age look and a thoroughly modern ride quality. <

MIKA AMARO
— Agravic Grey, Sapphire Black & Pearly White

From its workshop in Cologne, Germany, Mika Amaro produces premium, handmade bicycles for urban cyclists. As a German manufacturer and cycling enthusiast, founder **Michael Nagler's** top priority is quality. Each handcrafted Mika Amaro bike collection is limited to just III bikes per model; and each individual bike is tested to the smallest detail before delivery. Relying exclusively on durable and innovative components is at the core of Mika Amaro's philosophy. The bikes are only built with Gates Carbon Drives in combination with Shimano Alfine internal gear hubs, producing a maintenance-free, quiet, clean, light, and powerful ride. <

GILLES BERTHOUD
– Victor's Randonneur

French craftsman **Gilles Berthoud** and his workshop, Cycles Berthoud, designed the Randonneur for Victor, their rider in the Transcontinental Race. Although classic looking in design, the bike is completely modern in its use of technology. The frame features Reynolds 953 tubing, full internal wiring, a SON SL front dynamo hub (which charges the battery for the shifter), disc brakes, and as a highlight, the electronically-actuated Shimano Ultegra Di2. Many other parts were custom-made for the occasion, including the stainless steel front panniers rack, leather saddle, and superlight carbon fenders. <

ARKO BICI
– 650B Signature Randonneur XI

From his workshop in Cífer, Slovakia, designer **Marek Parajka** builds bespoke frames, stems, and racks that are both handcrafted and functional. The custom-built Signature Randonneur features a combination of classic geometry, stainless steel details, and a fillet-brazed, nickel-plated stem. The impressive frame is fitted with Campagnolo Veloce IIs, a Brooks saddle, Campagnolo Record headset, Grand Bois Hetre 650b tires, and Miche RC2 hubs. As a finishing touch for its proud Slovakian owner, Parajka embedded a vintage Slovak krone in the rear part of the stem. <

PASHLEY CYCLES
– Countryman, Guv'nor & Speed 5

Since 1926, Pashley Cycles has crafted quality bicycles from its workshop in Stratford-upon-Avon. As England's longest established bicycle manufacturer, the company's team designs and builds a unique range of traditional bicycles, using parts directly supplied by almost 100 British companies. From the Countryman to the exclusive Guv'nor Path Racer, each range includes classic and commuter bikes and retro beach cruisers. Pashley also supplies high-quality carrier cycles, cargo bikes, and load carrier tricycles for industrial and commercial use. <

– *Top:* The **Countryman**, which is
hand built from 531 steel tubing and
features Alfine 8 speed gears, is an ideal
companion on the daily commute.
– *Left:* The **Speed 5** a tribute to the
heyday of gentlemanly British cycle racing.

RETROCYCLE
– Velopedart

As a reinterpretation of the original Pedersen frame, designed by Danish designer **Mikael Pedersen** in 1890, the Velopedart combines classic and innovative elements for a new riding experience. Finding traditional saddles uncomfortable, Pedersen invented a new construction that smoothed bumpy rides by moving like a hammock. Velopedart, built by the Retrocycle bicycle manufactory in Lübeck, Germany, uses the same basic idea to create wave-like forward motion for the rider. The bike comes in four different frame sizes, with custom-made components. <

CHIOSSI CYCLES
– Maino

The history of Chiossi Cycles begins in 1942, when its founder **Enzo Chiossi** took a job as a bike shop boy of the legendary Ennio Gilli. Over the years, in collaboration with masters of the cycling world, the multigenerational company has produced bicycles that are inspired by a passion for racing and mechanics. This bike was originally a Maino frame from the 1940s featuring wooden Ghisallo rims with vintage Sturmey Archer hubs, with a front hub dynamo and internal wiring in the fork leg. The rear is a coaster brake with three speed hub gears operated by a Sturmey shifter. The crank set, possibly manufactured by Marinoni blends perfectly in the classic look. Today Paolo Chiossi and his colleagues design and build handcrafted bikes one by one in their workshop in Soliera, Italy. <

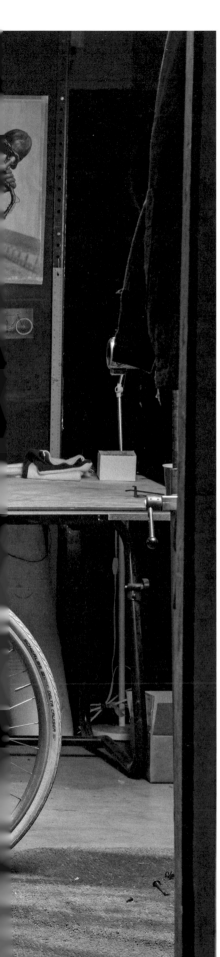

ASCARI BICYCLES
– The Ascari King Series

Founded in 2011 by designer **Helio Ascari** and his wife **Maria Thereza**, Ascari Bicycles specializes in custom bicycles with intricate detailing. The hand-brazed construction of the King series incorporates etched embellishments within the frame, fork, stem, and brake levers. All components are handbuilt from a variety of materials, including brass, bronze, aluminum, exotic woods, leather, gold, and precious gems. Ascari credits his Italian grandfather, a basket weaver by trade, for inspiring his signature leather-wrapping technique. <

– *Left:* Helio Ascari in his shop.
– *Above:* Bespoke grips, hubs, and frame details.

– *Left:* The **Ascari King Plus Black** comes with 13 optional ruby stones.
– *Top right:* Air pump and brake levers are custom built.
– *Above:* Crankset by Rene Herse and MKS pedals.
– *Bottom:* Details and logos in copper and brass are brazed onto the frame, fork, and stem.

WILLIAMSON GOODS & SUPPLY
– The Wheelmen Bicycle

Each Wheelmen bicycle is a custom-built master-piece, with lavish finishings and details. Hand-brazed in Detroit, using the highest quality chromoly tubing, the Wheelmen's frame, fork, lugs, and stem are all handmade by Williamson Goods & Supply with individual copper details and subtle logos brazed in place. Each compo-nent is wrapped with hand-sewn python or crocodile skin, while its brake levers, gear system, pedals, and cranks are assembled to the rider's exact specifications. <

GOCHIC BICYCLE
— YEE & Mini YEE

Drawing on his training as an automotive designer, Taipei-based **Alex Chou** combines technology with classic design in the Gochic YEE (28-inch wheels) and Mini YEE (24-inch wheels). The bike's unique lines echo France's Millau Viaduct bridge, while the seamless top tube extends into a basket holder that is perfect for light urban travel. Features include a lightweight 4130 Chromoly steel frame, a Gates Carbon belt-drive, and the option of SRAM 2- or 3-speed shifting. The grips and saddles are Gochic's own design. The Mini YEE has the same options as the YEE, but in a smaller package. Upgrades, such as disc brakes or a hand-polished finish, are left to the customer's choice. <

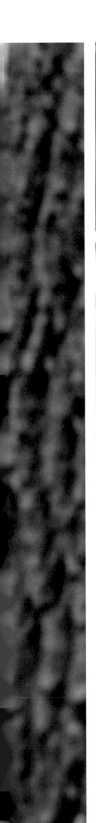

ECCE CYCLES
– Opus Cruise & Opus Sport

Founded in Brussels in 2012, ECCE partners with skilled engineers and craftsmen to create bicycles that are both original and technologically advanced. With its iconic double triangle form, ECCE Cycles forged a tradition of breaking the rules of urban bicycle design. Today, led by visionary designer **Pierre Lallemand**, ECCE Cycles produces bicycles that can also be viewed as works of art. <

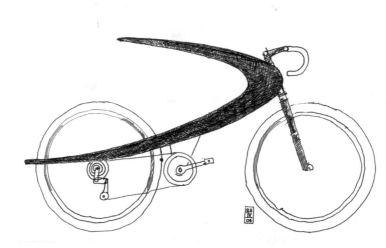

BY PIERRE LALLEMAND

– *Right:* The **Opus Sport** with a gloss finish and matte accessories.
– *Left and top:* The **Opus Cruise** combines leather parts with a carbon frame and polished 32 hole rims.

DIAMANT
– Juna Deluxe+ & Topas Villiger

Diamant's Juna Deluxe+ and Topas Villiger bikes offer new interpretations of its classic step-through frame. The Juna Deluxe+ is an e-bike with a Bosch Active engine, and a Purion controller, and a 250 W battery that can reach speeds of up to 15 mph (25 km/h). Its step-through aluminum frame has a retro design with classic lights, a front rack, hydraulic Tektro Vela disc brakes, and an integrated disc lock. The Topas Villager is a new version of the classic 1912 Diamant women's frame. In addition to its aluminum frame and rims, updates include an integrated disc lock, stainless mud guards, a comfortable seat, Shimano V-Brakes, and a Nexus 8 gear hub. The Topas Villager comes in three color choices: steel blue metallic, tofana white, and light blue. <

– *Left:* The **Topas Villiger** is the modern version of the classic 1912 Diamant stepthrough frame.
– *Top:* With its electric support that goes up to 15.5 mph (25 km/h), the Diamant **Juna Deluxe+** signals a new era.

CYCLE BOY
— *Apollo*

Chigasaki-based bicycle artist **Nobuyuki Tani** used to design cassette players, telephones, TV sets, and other technological classics for Sharp, but after leaving the company, he took over his father's small bicycle workshop "Cycle Boy," creating and designing custom bicycles with a mix of new and vintage parts. For the "Apollo" Tani was able to source a pile of new old stock parts like the light, grips and handlebars. The design is based on the Japanese Showa era with the main focus on practicality and durability. The proportions may look out of place, but the ride quality is not. <

CYCLE BOY
— Matiere

The Matiere features a compact step-through frame with a retro design that makes it perfect for city riding. Unlike mass-produced bicycles, **Nobuyuki Tani**'s bikes combine custom and vintage parts that give it a classic look and unique character. Even with its small tires, the Matiere's frame eliminates vibrations from the road, guaranteeing a comfortable ride. Celebrating pure materials, the compact bike features leather grips, a leather saddle, wooden mudguards and vintage stell pedals. In collaboration with design agency Ishinokura Shoten, three models (the Apollo, The Matiere and the Trunk) were created and produced as a limited edition. Tani's bicycle design for the movie "Kiki's Delivery Service" has even been displayed in the Chigasaki citizen gallery and art museum. <

MADE for the New JAPANESE Generation

For the style-conscious youth of greater Tokyo, a region with a population nearing 38 million, **Wachsen Bicycles** *offers beautifully customized transport solutions.*

In some of the more populous areas of the Tokyo metropolis, which itself has a population of approximately 14 million, simply riding a bike through the streets can be a challenge. Regardless of the staggering demographics, Tokyo still ranks at the top of every list of the world's most livable cities. Maybe it's the number of cars that Japan's capital has compared to other auto-centric cities like Los Angeles; the polite and helpful nature of its inhabitants is likely a contributing factor as well.

Despite the claustrophobic crowds, Tokyo is still a great city to cycle around. Bikes are an integral part of the culture—companies like Suzuki and Honda started building bicycles in their early days. The variety of

WACHSEN

The younger **GENERATION** of cyclists in Japan are influenced by excellent design, functionality, and— most importantly— **AFFORDABILITY.**

bikes on hand is in exact proportion to the aesthetic diversity of the citizens. You can spot everything from grossly expensive carbon fiber road bikes and colorfully accessorized ensembles to exquisitely restored vintage machines and unassuming bikes, all moving together to perform a multitude of daily tasks. From a commercial perspective, the market is huge. But Wachsen (German for "growing") Bicycles has discovered a niche: many members of the younger Japanese generation who ride are influenced by excellent design, functionality, and—importantly—affordability. The brand's bikes cater to such requirements. Drawing upon the country's many years of engineering experience, and inspired by ancient pursuits like bonsai, calligraphy, ikebana, and the martial arts, the Wachsen catalog can accommodate every

– *Top right:* The **Bango** is a retro 6-speed cargo bike with 26 inch wheels.
– *Left:* The **Grandy** is a fashionable cargo bike and perfect partner for shopping in Tokyo.
– *Right:* The compact 20 inch **Colot** cargo bike has stiff front and rear racks.

WACHSEN

– *Left and top:* The **Nicot**
with 24 inch wheels.
– *Top right:* The **Tragen**
is German for "carry."
– *Bottom right:* The **Roke**
painted in olive green.

customer's tastes. Wachsen's frames are constructed from both aluminum and steel, and are designed specifically with form and functionality in mind. The weight is kept to a minimum, and common features include a chain guard to protect the commuter's calves from grease marks. Integrated front or rear racks allow portage of essential light daily loads. Naturally, components are selected from the Shimano range of gear shifters, derailleurs, and brakes.

Ironically, the most striking feature is the subdued hues used in all the paint schemes on the bikes, in keeping with the local pared-down sensibility. There is no garish branding; color choices include olive, gray, and black monochromes, matched with retro gum-wall balloon tires, leather saddles, and handgrips. Perhaps it's the Japanese obsession with miniaturism, but the future of cycling in the capital is looking bright, thanks to Wachsen's collection of well-heeled bikes. <

WACHSEN'S FRAMES
are constructed from both **ALUMINUM** and steel.

Perhaps it's the Japanese OBSESSION with miniaturism, but the future of cycling in the capital is looking BRIGHT.

Named the **City Bike Klein**, this Japanese interpretation of the classic Dutch bike comes with a standard wooden basket.

WACHSEN

EIGHTY Years of ALEX SINGER Cycles

During the golden age of cycling, French constructeurs didn't just make frames, they crafted complete bicycles. The work of **Alex Singer**'s *shop is some of the most respected from that era.*

– *Left:* As grandson of the founder, Alex Singer, Olivier Csuka is keeping the tradition alive.
– *Top right:* The dark blue of the **Le Panaméen** is probably the signature colour of Alex Singer Cycles.

In post-war France, there were very few bicycle manufacturers, even in Paris, despite a rapidly increasing interest in the two-wheeled machines which offered citizens an inexpensive option for both commercial and recreational transport. Levallois-Perret was the center of the handmade car industry. As demand for bicycles grew, carriage works turned to the new trade for extra revenue. It was in this environment that Alex Singer, an ex-racer from Hungary who relocated to France in 1919, learned his craft.

At the time, factory-made components weren't available so the constructeurs made their own. To them, a bike wasn't just a frame but a cohesive unit with stems, seat posts, and racks integrated into the final ensemble. Singer was an incredible engineer who gained much respect for his bikes, some of which won awards at the Concours de Machines competition for their lightweight and robust construction. One of his tourers, for example, weighed less than 15 lbs (7 kg)—comparable with today's machines—even with accessories such as lights and fenders.

ALEX SINGER

– *Left:* Each bike is built specifically for the customer's needs. The randonneur comes with modern Dura-Ace shifting components and Grand Bois hubs. High tech brakes stop the bike on steep inclines.

The business still operates under the ALEX SINGER name today.

Singer founded his workshop in 1938, and worked alone, until he was joined by his nephew, Ernest Csuka, in 1944. The young apprentice introduced many innovations, modernized the bikes' geometries, and eventually took over the business in 1962, when Singer retired. Over the years, the number of orders fell, but then later increased, with many orders coming from fans in France, the U. S., and Japan. Sadly, Ernest died in December 2009, but not before he passed the torch and legacy to his son Olivier.

– *Left:* The rear light mount is a signature design detail.
Vintage parts mix with new retro-styled parts like the chrome racks.
– *Opposite left:* Singer also builds performance bikes
that mix classic steel frames with carbon wheels and modern
shifting components.
– *Opposite top:* A restored French classic by **August Sutter**.

ALEX SINGER

EPHEMERA and memorabilia from 80 years in BUSINESS cover the walls and shelves, giving the impression that time has stood still.

The business still operates under the Alex Singer name today, producing refined bicycles that are highly sought-after, especially in the Japanese market. There are currently six models available, ranging from the sporty Competition, Cyclosport Compact, and Course Prestige, to the Cyclotourisme Prestige randonneur, and long-distance Grand Tourisme. The Ile-de-France is a nostalgic

The bike specifically built for the famous Paris-Brest-Paris race.

racer that rides as well as any modern carbon frame, albeit with a lot more integrity and everyday practicality.

Alex Singer Cycles also performs restorations of steel frames. The company's new bikes are still made by hand in the back room of 53 Rue Victor Hugo, Levallois-Perret, where visitors are invited to come and absorb the stories and emotions which reside within the workshop. The walls and shelves are covered with the ephemera and memorabilia of 80 years in business, giving visitors the unmistakable impression that time has stood still. With today's bicycle culture racing ahead at the pace of a derby, that might just be a welcome relief. <

– *Top:* Beautifully executed brake lines move along the frame.
– *Right:* Smoothed out frame details.

CHAPMAN CYCLES
– Deb's mixte basket bike

The front basket and step-through frame of the coral-colored mixte basket bike for Deb were just a few of the custom design decisions made by **Brian Chapman** of Providence-based Chapman Cycles. Uneven city streets go virtually unnoticed underneath the bike's 1.65 in (42 mm) Grand Bois tires, while its fully-integrated pump, fenders, and generator lights make riding enjoyable in all weather conditions. A Schmidt Edelux headlight with daylight sensor and a rear vintage Miller light (retrofitted with an LED bulb) make night riding both safe and easy. The drivetrain is a minimal 1 × 9, with a Shimano 105 rear derailleur and a Velo Orange crankset with a custom-machined chain guard. <

INDEX

INDEX

VELO CITY

This book was conceived, edited, and designed by Gestalten.

Edited by **Robert Klanten and Maximilian Funk**

Preface by **Erik Spiekermann**
Project texts by **Rebecca Silus**
Profile texts by **Adam Leddin**
Expert essays by **Andrea Casalotti, Jenni Gwiazdowski,
Nora Manthey and James Thoem**

Project Management by **Sam Stevenson**

Creative Direction of Design by **Ludwig Wendt**
Design and Layout by **Léon Giogoli**
Layout assistance by **Stefan Morgner and Mona Osterkamp**
Cover by **Jan Blessing**

Typefaces: Priori Sans by **Jonathan Barnbrook**

Cover photography by **Marc Pillai**

Printed by **Printer Trento S. R. L., Trento, Italy**
Made in Europe

Published by Gestalten, Berlin 2018
ISBN 978-3-89955-654-4

Bibliographic information published by the Deutsche
Nationalbibliothek.
The Deutsche Nationalbibliothek lists this publication in
the Deutsche Nationalbibliografie; detailed bibliographic
data are available online at http://dnb.d-nb.de.

None of the content in this book was published in exchange
for payment by commercial parties or designers;
Gestalten selected all included work based solely on its
artistic merit.
This book was printed on paper certified according to the
standards of the FSC®.